# SAFE AS HOUSES?

# SAFE AS HOUSES?

## A Historical Analysis
of Property Prices

Neil Monnery

LONDON PUBLISHING PARTNERSHIP

Published by London Publishing Partnership,
Bon Marché Centre, 241–251 Ferndale Road,
London SW9 8BJ, UK

www.londonpublishingpartnership.co.uk

ISBN-13: 978-1-907994-01-2 (pbk.)

A catalogue record for this book is available from the British Library

This book has been composed in Palatino using LATEX

Copyedited and typeset by T&T Productions Ltd, London
www.tandtproductions.com

Printed in the United Kingdom by Hobbs the Printers Ltd

# CONTENTS

# INTRODUCTION

A COUPLE OF YEARS AGO I was asked to become a trustee of a local charity. It had successfully survived for hundreds of years, making it one of Britain's oldest charities. A key role for the trustees was to set the investment approach, with the aim that the charity would continue to prosper for the next few hundred years. This presented the trustees with a dilemma: most of the assets were local residential property. On the one hand, this strategy had delivered very attractive returns over the previous decade, but on the other, the approach seemed to go against the logic of diversifying risk. The issue had been much discussed and as a new trustee I was asked my thoughts. To buy some time I suggested I would have a think about it.

And so I started to write a paper that became the genesis of this book. In it I tried to assess how houses had performed *as an investment*. I was surprised, however, by just how difficult it was to get hold of data describing the returns to owning a house over a long period of time – much more difficult than it was to get the equivalent data for shares or bonds. It struck me as odd that there was such patchy data for what is the most important investment that the majority of people will make in their lives.

I set about searching through libraries, ordering out-of-print books and scouring obscure corners of the internet in search of longer-run data series on house prices. For that initial paper I found a couple of series that stretched back hundreds of years and the findings seriously challenged my preconceptions. Because the results were not what I had expected, I kept digging and eventually found enough unexpected results that my thoughts turned to putting them down in a book.

*Safe As Houses?* takes the data that I have gathered together from across countries and through history and compares it with what people think about house prices in the UK today.

For most of us our house is also our home. Our reason for purchasing a house is as much to do with our lifestyles and our needs as it is to do with making an investment, but when we do purchase a house, we *are* making a major investment. As I thought about people's attitude to that investment in housing, it seemed to me that there is a collective set of beliefs, and they can be summarized as follows.

- House prices go up over the medium and long term.

- Dips are an opportunity to get into the market because they are relatively brief.

- Prices grow well ahead of the rate of inflation, making houses a very good investment.

These beliefs are rationally derived from the experience of the housing market that we have had over our lifetimes. But many of us have a slight nervousness about whether these beliefs will continue to hold true over the next few decades: the world seems more uncertain; there are some worrying stories about property price declines elsewhere in the world; and, as we know all too well, if house prices do turn, we can be left in real difficulty, with some facing repossession and even bankruptcy.

You can see this uncertainty in the very low current levels of house sales, as buyers and sellers pause to assess where the market might head next. Some wonder whether this dip is different from previous ones: as prices fall will this present an opportunity to buy into the market at an attractive level or is there, as some others believe, a chance that the future will look very different from our experience of the last ten or twenty years?

As shares in railway companies crashed in the UK in the 1860s, the phrase 'as safe as houses' entered the lexicon.[1] Given the timing, some argue that it promoted the virtues of property as a solid investment in troubled times, but others argue that this interpretation has been grafted onto a phrase that actually referred to physical safety – a family of phrases that started in the 1600s with 'as safe as a mouse in a mill' and moved on to 'as safe as a crow in a gutter' before reaching 'as safe as houses'.[2] Others argue that 'safe' in eighteenth-century English simply meant 'certain'.[3] Even the phrase 'as safe as houses' needs some examination if we are to fully understand it – and as we will see, so too does our understanding of house prices.

In this book we will look at how house prices have moved in many countries around the world: from America in the west to Japan in the east, and from Norway in the north to Australia in the south. We will also look across history and see how wars, economic growth, plagues, population growth, inflation and many other factors have affected house prices in these different countries. It will become clear how difficult it is to make simple predictions on where the housing market might head.

This book tries to provide a broad and long-term perspective on the way in which property values behave. It discusses some of the implications of those changes, both at a personal level for us as individuals and families wanting to own our own home and also on a wider level given the way in which house prices can affect the economy and the society in which we live.

**CHAPTER 1**

---

# ARE WE AS SAFE AS HOUSES?

### A TOPIC FOR DISCUSSION?

How OFTEN DO YOU SEE a headline in the newspaper about house prices? Or take a moment to look in an estate agent's window? Or chat with a neighbour about the price of a local house that has just sold? House prices are famously the theme of many an idle conversation, but they are of course much more than this.

For most people, the biggest purchase we will ever make is our house. It will usually be our largest investment and represent the greatest part of our wealth. The level of house prices will determine if we can buy a house in the course of our lives and, if we can, when. Those same prices will affect how much we need to borrow and pay back, heavily influencing our standard of living. And how prices rise and fall may determine the level of resources we have to fall back on in old age.[1] It seems that house price rises also have a positive effect on our happiness, with rising house prices making us more optimistic about the future.[2] Given all of this, it is perhaps surprising that we do not talk about house prices even more.

For most people, buying a house is a long-term commitment. Typically, after we have bought a house we stay in it for over a decade before moving, and once we start owning we tend to remain owners for most of our lives.[3] You cannot easily and effortlessly trade in and out of owning a house. And yet there are a small number of key decision points in our lives where reflection about house prices is of particular value. These might revolve around when to buy, whether to trade up or down, whether to put more money into housing via buy-to-let, how much debt to take on, and the like. Make these decisions well and prosperity may follow, make them badly and the consequences can be devastating.

For most people their house is also their home, and it is hard to separate the investment element of house ownership from the day-to-day need for a home in which to live. And yet it is a critical and consequential investment decision.

With average earnings in the UK currently around £26,500 before tax and approximately £20,000 after tax, a forty-year working career would produce around £800,000 of lifetime after-tax earnings in today's money.[4] With the average house costing around £165,000 you can quickly see that a very large part of our working life is devoted to creating the capital required to own a home.[5] Even at today's artificially low interest rates, mortgage holders are paying an average of 20% of their income to service their mortgages.[6] For that reason, the purchase of a house should not be entered into unadvisedly, lightly or wantonly, but advisedly, knowingly and soberly.

And with high levels of ownership in most countries, most of us are now directly affected by house prices. At the end of the First World War, just over 20% of homes in the UK were owned by their occupants, with most people renting. Now nearly 70% of homes are owner-occupied.

This rise in the proportion of owner–occupiers has occurred in all developed countries around the world, so that home ownership rates are now typically between 50% and 80%, with a fair degree of variation, as can be seen in table 1.1. As we will see, this variation may affect how the housing market is seen in different countries and the way in which changes in house prices affect those economies more generally.

**Table 1.1.** Home ownership rates by country, 2009.

| | |
|---|---|
| Spain | 85% |
| Belgium | 78% |
| Norway | 77% |
| Ireland | 75% |
| Australia | 70% |
| UK | 69% |
| US | 67% |
| Canada | 67% |
| France | 57% |
| Germany | 43% |

*Data source*: EMF.[7]

As we are increasingly aware, changes in the housing market can lead to changes in the financial markets and the real economy. We have seen that rising house prices can lead to people remortgaging to boost their spending and, through that, the level of consumption in the economy as a whole. We have also seen how fragile the banks are when their loans start to go wrong.

And now, for the first time ever, the level of house ownership has stalled as the historically high house prices have made it difficult for many to buy.[8] This is particularly the case for the young, many of whom currently rent but have historically aspired to own their own home in due course.[9] With recent price rises, however, many are beginning to wonder if they will ever be able to buy.[10]

For individuals, for the economy and for society, house prices matter. But despite this, we know surprisingly little about house prices, and what we do know is based on relatively limited information. This chapter (and this book) will dig deeper.

**SEEING IS BELIEVING**

Our experience of the housing market depends on where and when we were born. As we will see when we look at other countries over different time periods, the experience of owning a house is extremely varied. In the UK, first-time buyers might be in their mid–late thirties and they can look forward to forty-plus years of ownership. The *average* homeowner would be in their early fifties, would have purchased their first home twenty-plus years ago, when they were about thirty years old, and can expect a further twenty-plus years of ownership. Older homeowners might have bought in the early 1960s, with some venerable owners having climbed onto the property ladder in the 1950s.

So the period from the 1950s to the present day spans our collective experience. This is an experience that has forged the way we tend to think about house prices. The result is that most of us have come to hold three beliefs about the housing market. We might summarize them as follows: first, that house prices mostly go up; second, that dips are relatively brief and represent an opportunity to get onto the housing ladder; and third, that a house is a very good investment that will materially outperform inflation and other types of asset. Let us look at these three beliefs in more detail.

### 'OUR EXPERIENCE SHOWS THAT HOUSE PRICES GO UP' (MOST OF THE TIME)

So, what has happened to house prices over this period of time? When a headline announces a change in house prices in the UK, it is usually reporting the findings of one of the six main house price indices,[11] the most regularly quoted of which are the Halifax House Price Index and the Nationwide House Price Index. These two mortgage providers collect data from their own lending operations and, using a technique known as the hedonic approach, their statisticians adjust the prices for these properties to get to an estimate for an average property.[12] If, for instance, a house included in their calculations has two garages but the average house has only one, the statisticians will take away the added value of the second garage to create an estimate for the price of a

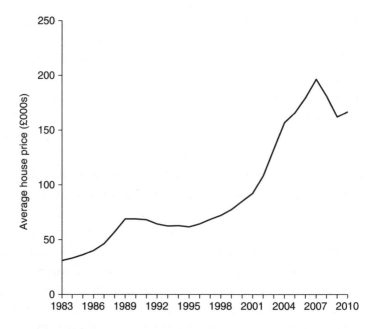

**Figure 1.1.** Halifax House Price Index, 1983–2010.
*Data source*: Halifax.

'standard' house. This estimate is then compared with previous periods to come up with an index of prices over time.*

Articles normally only report a year-on-year figure, or if they include a historical chart, it typically only goes back a few years. But the data is available for much longer periods. The Halifax House Price Index, which is shown in figure 1.1, goes back to 1983, and so is a good representation of the experience of our average homeowner. The picture it shows is a dramatic rise in the price of an average house: from around £31,000 in 1983 to around £165,000 today.

---

*In 2010, Halifax noted that the number of households lacking an inside toilet had fallen from 14% in 1960 to 0.2% in 1996, that the number of houses without hot water had fallen from 22% in 1967 to 1% in 1991, and that the number of homes with central heating had increased from 35% in 1971 to 92% in 2000. Detached houses made up 10% of all new homes built between 1945 and 1961 but 36% of those built after 1980.[13]

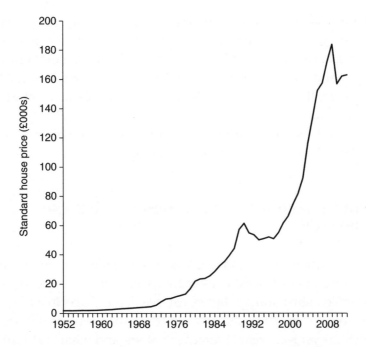

**Figure 1.2.**  Nationwide House Price Index, 1952–2010.
*Data source*: Nationwide.

There was a period when prices fell after the recession of the early 1990s, but either side of that period prices rose considerably. Even when we take into account the current dip caused by the global financial crisis that started in 2007, prices are still nearly five times higher than they were twenty-five years ago.

We can get an even longer perspective for the UK by looking at the Nationwide House Price Index (shown in figure 1.2), which provides figures stretching back to 1952. This index covers the full period of our collective experience – that is, the period over which almost every homeowner alive today has been active in the housing market. The story it tells is even more dramatic.

In 1952 the price of a house was around £1,900, compared with around £165,000 today. Our older homeowner, who bought their house in the early 1960s for around £2,500, has seen a near seventyfold increase in the value of their home. Our average homeowner, who bought in the late 1980s when prices had reached around £40,000, has seen a near fourfold increase. In fact, unless someone bought and sold between 1990 and 1995 or purchased in the last few years, they are likely to be feeling very satisfied with their investment.

Given this experience it is not surprising that we have come to believe that house prices tend to go up.

### 'OUR EXPERIENCE SUGGESTS DIPS ARE BRIEF AND SHALLOW'

Of course, there are times when prices have fallen. There have also been a number of periods over the years when the growth rate has slowed temporarily. But we can see in the charts that after the plateaux and the dips, the upward trend soon returns. Figure 1.3 shows the year-on-year changes in values, and what is striking is that prices rarely fall. Indeed there are only two negative spells: the early 1990s recession and the recent fall in 2008–9.

Most people have taken this to mean that price drops are short-lived, and that the trend quickly reasserts itself. This has led to our second belief: that dips are an opportunity to get into the market before it restarts its ascent.

To examine our third belief – that houses are a good investment – we will need to look at their performance over similar periods of time compared with inflation and with other types of investment.

### 'OUR EXPERIENCE IS THAT PRICES BEAT INFLATION' (BUT BY LESS THAN YOU MAY THINK)

We all know that the pound in your pocket today is not the same as the pound of the 1960s given the effects of inflation. The reason for starting with the nominal prices above is that that is how we instinctively think about house prices.

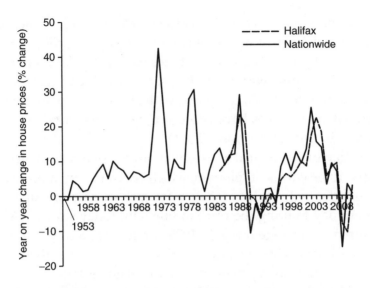

**Figure 1.3.** Year-on-year change in house prices.
*Data sources*: Nationwide; Halifax.

When my family moved into our current house about a decade ago, we thought we had done rather well because our old house had increased in value by two-and-a-half times over the ten years we had owned it. One of our new neighbours, who had moved into their house thirty years before, thought they had done rather better in that their house had increased in value by fourteen times over the thirty years they had lived in it. As if to put us all to shame, another neighbour noted that their house was now worth about forty times what they had paid for it fifty years previously. But all of us were doing these calculations using nominal prices. We all knew that the data ignored the effects of inflation, but we somehow suspended our thinking about inflation for the purpose of this calculation – perhaps because it would be difficult, perhaps because we wanted to think of the rise in the most favourable terms, in order to show our investment prowess.

When we talk about other things that we buy, we are quick to incorporate the effects of inflation, and these effects are large. Take the humble pint of beer as an example. In 1960 a pint cost eight or nine pence. By 1982 it had soared to fifty-eight pence. In a London pub today it will usually cost three pounds for a pint – if you are lucky. It costs thirty-five times more than it did fifty years ago. It is the same with many items: a loaf of bread cost around two pence in the 1950s compared with around one pound today. Fortunately, as prices have risen so too have incomes – in 1982, average income was around £7,000.

To get a sense of 'real' (post-inflation) house prices we need to strip out the effects of inflation, which we can do by multiplying house price by the rate of inflation for each year leading up to the present day to bring the price in line with today's prices. As an example, an average house in 1975 would have cost you around £10,000, but because the price of goods has risen over time at the rate of inflation, to buy the same amount of goods today as £10,000 would have bought you in 1975, you would need to have £75,000 in your pocket. So, while the *nominal* price of a house in 1975 was £10,000, the *real* price, in today's money, was £75,000.

When we buy something and hold it for a number of years, as we do with a house, we tend to lose track of the small yearly changes. In some cases this can lead us to think that prices have risen – when in fact the *real* price has hardly changed at all.

We can look at the Nationwide house price index on a *real* (inflation-adjusted) basis, and the real prices are shown in figure 1.4. This looks like a compressed version of the *nominal* house price graph we saw earlier, and although the shape is much the same, the changes in real prices are much less dramatic than the nominal price changes that we saw above. In today's money, house prices have risen from around £42,000 in 1952 to around £165,000 today – a still substantial, but more modest, quadrupling of values. Given this we can see that real house prices have risen ahead of inflation over the last fifty-plus years.

When we look at real house prices, two more dips emerge. In 1974 oil prices quadrupled, causing both a recession and a spike in the rate of inflation. House prices increased more slowly than general inflation between 1974 and 1977, falling over 30% in real

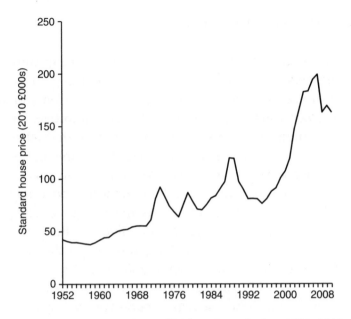

**Figure 1.4.** Nationwide Real House Price Index, 1952–2010.
*Data sources*: Nationwide; ONS.[14]

terms. The recession in the early years of the Thatcher government also caused real house prices to fall by nearly 20% between 1979 and 1982.

Compare for a moment 1997 with 1987. Here the real prices are roughly the same, at between £80,000 and £90,000. But if we just looked at the nominal price graph, we would say that prices had risen by one-third from £45,000 to £60,000. This is the illusion that can be created if we look only at nominal prices – an illusion of wealth creation when we are really doing no more than keeping up with inflation.

Nevertheless, the overall message from the index is that *real* house prices do rise. The dips are more dramatic, and it suggests that greater care needs to be taken in seizing on these dips as a buying opportunity; but when purchases are well timed, the growth of real prices suggests that over the last fifty years, house prices comfortably beat inflation.

## EINSTEIN AND HOUSE PRICES

Some people claim that Einstein once said that the greatest force in the universe was the power of compounding. (Others assert equally strongly that he said nothing of the sort.) Compounding, as we will see, can be a powerful, and counterintuitive, force.

To illustrate this, there is a famous parable that tells of the servant who invented the game of chess. When the prince offers him any reward he would like, he asks the prince to put one grain of rice on the first square, double that on the second, double that on the third and so on until the sixty-fourth square. The prince agrees. It starts gently enough: for the first row, the prince puts down 1, 2, 4, 8, 16, 32, 64 and 128 grains. But at the end of the second row when he puts down 32,768 grains on the sixteenth square he is probably sweating. Halfway through, on the thirty-second square, the prince faces the prospect of needing two billion grains of rice, and by the time the last square is reached, the prince requires nine million trillion grains.*

This is the power of compounding, which captures the idea that as the value of something goes up, the next increase applies to that increased value so that small increments can become huge differences over time. It is this that (perhaps) so awed Einstein. It applies to house prices in large part because we keep our houses for long periods of time, and also because with inflation the nominal growth rates are quite high. If something grows at 7% per year, it will double in value every ten years. And as the prince discovered, doublings soon add up.

Going back to my experience with my neighbours, my old house was valued at two-and-a-half times the amount I had paid only ten years earlier: that is an annual growth rate of 9.5%. The thirty-year resident, whose house rose in value fourteenfold in thirty years enjoyed a 9.1% growth rate, while the fifty-year

---

*Mathematically, the second square gets 2 grains, the third gets $2^2$ grains, the eighth gets $2^7$ grains, and so on. By the sixty-fourth square, there are $2^{63}$ grains: 9,223,000,000,000,000,000 grains.

resident, whose house's value went up fortyfold in fifty years enjoyed a 7.6% growth rate.

These figures are before stripping out inflation. Doing that totally changes the story: our house rose at around 6% annually in real terms, that of my thirty-year neighbour rose by 3.3%, and that of the fifty-year resident by only 1.7%. This was no reflection on my investment skills of course; as we will see, real prices have risen very rapidly in recent years, and at a much faster rate than they have at any other time in the UK.

Let us look again at the Nationwide House Price Index (see figure 1.5). In the Real House Price Index, you will see that there is a trend line showing that, on average, *real* prices have risen by 2.4% each year.* This does not sound nearly as impressive as the statement that the average house bought in 1952 for £1,900 is now worth around £165,000, and it is not as dramatic as the chessboard parable, but a real growth rate of 2.4% does compound powerfully over longer periods. Over the same period, real Gross Domestic Product (GDP) per capita has increased more slowly at only 1.4% per year, so house prices not only outstripped inflation but also economic growth too.[15]

The simple maths of compounding gives us a reason why house prices cannot keep increasing at the rate that they have been. Recently, real house prices have been increasing at over 5% each year; meanwhile, the economy has grown around 2% each year after inflation. If this difference of 3% between economic growth and house price growth were to continue for a century, the average house would cost around £22 million in today's money, while average annual earnings would have risen to around £145,000 after tax. A mortgage at a rate of 5% would eat up over a million pounds in interest charges per year.† For this reason, most

---

*A good way to visually accommodate compound growth is to use a logarithmic scale. With such a scale a constant percentage increase plots as a straight line. A set of logarithmic scaled charts are included in appendix A for those that prefer this.

†Even at 3% house price growth (i.e. 1% ahead of GDP growth), the price of the average house would be over £3 million a century from now. Mortgage payments at a rate of 5% would be £155,000 per year – still ahead of after-tax income.

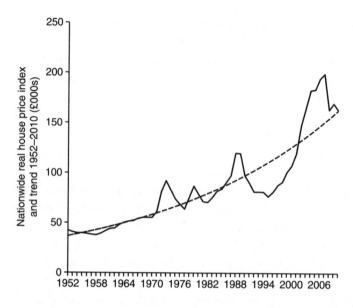

**Figure 1.5.** Nationwide Real House Price Index and trend, 1952–2010.
*Data sources*: Nationwide; ONS.

economists agree that over the long term house prices cannot grow faster than the economy for an indefinite period. And if you believe that, then the recent rates of growth in house prices are unsustainable.

## HOUSES VERSUS OTHER INVESTMENTS

Now that we have established that house prices have risen ahead of inflation, the next belief to examine is that a house is a good investment. So, how does an investment in a house, with a long-term annual real return of 2.4% each year, and an overall increase of ninetyfold since 1952, compare with an investment in other assets?

Rather surprisingly, if instead of buying an average house in 1952 you had invested £1,900 in equities and reinvested the dividends, it would now be worth around £2 million.[16] The same

**Table 1.2.** Investment returns since 1952.

|  | Inflation | Houses (real) | Equities (real) | Gilts (real) |
|---|---|---|---|---|
| 1952–2010 | 5.5% | 2.4% | 6.9% | 1.9% |
| 1980–2010 | 4.0% | 2.5% | 7.9% | 5.9% |
| 1995–2010 | 2.8% | 5.2% | 3.8% | 4.3% |

*Data source*: Barclays Equity Gilt Study (2011).

amount invested in gilts would have produced a rather less impressive £130,000. So we can see that houses have not been the only remarkable investment of the last few decades – but bear in mind that if you had invested everything in equities you may have had nowhere to live.

Equities have increased a thousandfold in just under sixty years. But, of course, we must strip out inflation. This makes the increase drop to a more modest fiftyfold increase. If we go further and adjust for compounding, we can calculate that equities produced an average annual return of 6.9% in real terms, as shown in table 1.2.

It will surprise many people that an investment in the stock market would have outperformed the increase in value they have seen in their house. For a full comparison we would need to incorporate fees,* tax and, most significantly, the benefit of living in the house without paying rent. An estimate of this might be a gross yield (rent before expenses) of around 4%, and a net yield (after expenses such as repairs, letting fees, transaction costs and so on) of around 2.5%. Adding this to the real price increase of 2.4% over

---

*Nowadays, with low-cost tracker funds those fees for equities might be around 0.5% but that would have been hard to achieve over this period. The effect fees have in sapping returns is enormous. One hundred pounds earning 4% in real terms will become £710 in fifty years, giving a gain of £610. Reduce that by paying 2% fees and the gain will fall to £169: this fall of about three-quarters in your gain when you halve the rate of return is another trick of compounding. The heavy charges that sap returns have led to the establishment of trackers to give investors a fairer deal.[17] It is estimated that in Britain we pay £413 million each day to those managing our investments.[18] If you were unable to avoid such high fee levels this would make a house a better long-term investment.

the period gives a return of just over 5%, which is much closer to the returns on equities.

In addition, houses are the only investment that most of us make using leverage – with some lenders providing 90% of the finance. If, say, you bought a £160,000 house with a 20% deposit, you would need £32,000 plus a mortgage of £128,000. Assume that house prices rise at a nominal 7% per year (4% real plus 3% inflation) for twenty years and assume that you pay the mortgage interest but make no capital repayments. In twenty years' time your house is worth £620,000 and your mortgage is still £128,000. Your equity has increased from your £32,000 deposit to £492,000 (£620,000 minus the £128,000 mortgage), which is a compound annual return of more than 14% per year. Try suggesting to your bank manager that you would like to make a similarly leveraged investment in the stock market!

While a 20% increase in house prices doubles our equity value, a 20% decline wipes us out. The leverage machine that produces remortgaging opportunities is the same leverage machine that drives repossessions. And it is at such a time that we realize that our house is an investment as well as a home. In the last few decades, during which prices have generally risen, this extra leverage has worked greatly to our advantage.

It turns out that both houses and equities have been excellent investments over the last forty or fifty years. Equities have outperformed an investment in housing on an unleveraged basis, but for the majority of people who could leverage property but not equities, leveraged property has outperformed unleveraged equities. This effect is even more dramatic in the last ten to fifteen years as real house price growth has increased and real equity returns have decreased.

## OUR BELIEFS ARE CONDITIONED BY OUR EXPERIENCE

Altogether, the three beliefs about house prices that we have built up through our collective experience seem to be supported by the available data from the last sixty years. Given our experience, it is no surprise that we think that

- house prices go up over the medium and long term,

- dips are an opportunity to get into the market because these dips are relatively brief, and

- prices grow well ahead of the rate of inflation, making houses a very good investment.

So long as you were not unlucky with your timing, over the last two generations buying houses has been, as the name of this book suggests, as *safe as houses*. This has been particularly true in the last fifteen years, when house prices have been increasing at a rate that has exceeded even our past benchmarks, having increased at more than twice the longer-term annual real rate.

### BUT WILL THE MUSIC STOP?

Can house prices really keep rising forever? Is there a limit to how fast they can grow? Have we just lived through an atypical period? There are a number of worrying signs.

House prices have begun to fall in the UK and are around 10% down in nominal terms and nearly 20% down in real terms from their 2007 peak. As we look around the world, we can see major falls in many countries, and we might naturally wonder if the same will happen here. While some forecasters predict a flattening of house prices, others are predicting falls of 20–50%. We worry that with interest rates at an all time low, the potential is there for property prices to be hit as rates start to rise. And we can see inflation emerging that may quietly erode the value of our houses.

The number of house sales has fallen by over a half, as have new mortgage approvals. Buyers appear unwilling to pay the prices that are being asked and sellers are sitting tight, waiting to see if the market rises. In the auction market, where a price has to be found, transactions are taking place at prices about 25%

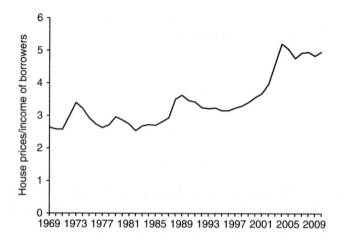

**Figure 1.6.** Ratio of house prices to incomes of borrowers in the UK. *Data source*: DCLG English Housing Survey.[19]

below the level of the normal market, having been stable at around the same level as the normal market from 1998 to 2007.[20]

Many are concerned that housing is still less affordable than in the past, as is illustrated by the ratio of house prices to the income of borrowers, which has reached a high of around five-to-one (see figure 1.6). Some are unsure how future generations will be able to pay the ever increasing prices for housing.[21]

### DOES IT MATTER?

Where house prices head will affect us all as individuals, as an economy and as a society.

As individuals we are directly affected by house prices. If the average house is worth around £165,000, a 25% increase in house prices will add over £40,000 to its value – about two years of average post-tax income. A 25% fall wipes £40,000 off the value of the house and would put many into negative equity or worse. Across the country, the houses we own are worth around £4,000 billion.*

*For this book a billion will mean 1,000 million and a trillion is 1,000 billion.

But about 60% of houses have mortgages, which in total add up to a debt of over £1,200 billion – money that is owed to the banks. The share that we truly own is therefore worth around £2,800 billion. If house prices were to increase by 25%, that would add £1,000 billion to the wealth of house-owners. If house prices were to fall by 25%, the same amount of wealth would evaporate. Given that our annual GDP is £1,400 billion, the gaining or losing of a trillion is a big deal.

This unease over the future of the economy and of house prices is changing our attitude to borrowing and spending. When house prices were on a seemingly unstoppable rise in the late 1990s and early 2000s, many in the UK were using their gains to finance holidays, cars, home improvements, their children's education and their retirements. In the peak year of 2006 British homeowners remortgaged their homes to the tune of £50 billion, boosting their spending power and adding nearly 6% to households' post-tax income.[22] Over the period from 1997 to 2007, we remortgaged our homes by over £300 billion. But it now looks as if many of us are uneasy about our levels of debt: last year we reduced our mortgage debts by a record £25 billion. This in turn is reducing spending.

Beyond the effect on individual spending, the banking sector is heavily exposed to the fortunes of the housing market. With £1,200 billion of outstanding loans secured against the value of our houses, banks' balance sheets would be tipping dangerously towards insolvency if people began struggling to pay these loans. In the current financial crisis we have seen how the banks' leveraged positions in the housing market, particularly in the US, have contributed to financial turmoil and played a part in causing a recession of a magnitude not seen since the 1930s.* If even 5% of

*The issue of bank leverage (how much they lend versus how much equity they have) has moved from being a topic for regulators' conferences to become a regular feature of newspaper stories. At the height of the current crisis many banks lent over twenty times their equity – meaning that if 5% of those loans defaulted, they were bankrupt. Much of the discussion about how to avoid a future crisis revolves around reducing leverage ratios and increasing equity ratios so that banks can withstand a higher level of default.[23]

the mortgage debt was impaired, it would wipe £25 billion off the balance sheets of Britain's banks, making them weaker and less able to lend.

Movements in house prices not only affect our individual prosperity, and through that our national economy, but such changes also have some hidden effects on our society, and in particular on how wealth is spread between generations. If we take the houses that existed fifteen years ago, between then and now they have increased in value by over £2,500 million in nominal terms and by around £1,800 million in real terms. This huge increase in our wealth at first seems like the mythical free lunch – gains without any losers. But there have been many losers: all the people who want to buy houses in the future and who will have to pay these higher prices. The rise in house prices over this period represents a real gain to house-owners of £1,800 million, and a loss of future income of the same amount for future house-owners.

A decade ago, over 40% of people in the UK under the age of thirty owned a house with a mortgage, but this has now dropped to below 30%. Indeed, one of the most striking statistics that emerges from studying the housing market is how much older the average first-time buyer has become. In 1977, the average first-time buyer was aged twenty-seven, by 2007 this had risen to thirty-four, and now it stands at around thirty-seven.[24]

These are huge changes in the demographics of house ownership, largely driven by the fact that over the last few decades the rise in house prices has exceeded the growth in people's earnings. This rise in house prices may affect our lives in indirect ways too. With many feeling that they need to buy houses as soon as they can to get a foot on the property ladder, they may end up settling for a smaller house, or one further from work and having a long commute rather than choosing to rent closer to their work; they may delay marriage and having children until they can buy a suitable home; they may need to reduce spending elsewhere to finance their mortgages.

Politicians are increasingly attuned to how the distribution of wealth, and in particular housing wealth, varies by age groups.

If house prices had increased at only 1% ahead of inflation since 1995, current house-purchasers would be paying around £60,000 less than they are. Put another way, the younger buyer needs to work an extra three years or so to be able to buy their house from the older homeowner. In his book *The Pinch: How the Baby Boomers Took Their Children's Future – And Why They Should Give It Back*,[25] David Willets, a government minister, points out just how much the older generations own of the wealth that exists in the UK.* He sees this concentration as a problem and as a possible cause for future intergenerational conflict.

As is now clear, different levels of increases in house prices create different winners and losers. But because very few new houses are built in any year (typically well below 1% of the stock of existing houses), changes in value produce only minor changes in the number of houses, or the state of housing stock. In reality, price rises and price falls create huge transfers of wealth between those who own a house and those who will own a house in the future.† It is for this reason, amongst others, that government policy cannot be indifferent to where house prices are going.

As the next few years unfold, we will see if 2011 was merely a pause on the steady upward rise of house values. If it proves to be just that, this would be entirely consistent with the experience we have had over our lifetimes in the UK. Or maybe we will come to see that, for various reasons, the beliefs that we have built up over our lifetimes are somehow incomplete. The aim of the next few chapters is to bring the experiences of others to bear as we contemplate that question.

We will go on a tour that will take us through centuries of war, peace, breakouts of plague, discoveries of gold, revolutions

---

*Willets estimates that the ownership of assets by age group is roughly split: 34%, over sixty-fives; 52%, those aged between forty-five and sixty-five; and 13%, under forty-fives.

†Another interesting finding from behavioural finance is that we care much more about losing something we already have than we do about losing something that we *could* have. This is one reason why we will hear a lot from the losers if house prices fall but very little from the winners. This asymmetry may also have a political consequence.

– bloodless or otherwise – recessions, depressions, rent controls, asset bubbles, bank failures, construction booms and miracles of human development. We will look back at how house prices have changed over the past hundred years in the US, Norway and Australia, over the past four hundred years in Amsterdam and over the past eight hundred years in Paris. We will also look at recent stories from Germany, Japan, Sweden, Ireland and Spain. All of these will shed some light on our experience in the UK. Our first stop on this journey will be the US, where owning a house has been anything but a smooth ride.

# CHAPTER 2

# AMERICAN DREAMS AND NIGHTMARES

## STARTING AT THE TOP

IF WE ARE GOING TO begin looking at house prices, it might be appropriate to start at the top. The world's most famous house in the world's largest and most powerful economy: the White House. With its own underground bunker designed to withstand a nuclear blast, we might also call it the safest. But has it been a safe investment?

When Irish architect James Hoban finished the house in 1800, the value was said to be around $230,000, which at today's prices would be around $3 million.

According to Zillow (an online housing marketplace), the value of the White House has risen more than eighty times over and stands at around $250 million today. When George W. Bush took up residence in 2001, the White House was valued at nearly $170 million but when he handed over the keys to Barack Obama the house was estimated to be worth just over $300 million. If we accept these valuations, the value of the White House nearly doubled in those eight years. Since then, however, it has fallen back, together with much of the American housing market.[1]

The White House's rise from $230,000 in 1800 to today's
$250,000,000 in nominal terms is equivalent to a rise from $3 million to $250 million in real terms. Because this rise took place over
210 years, it represents an annual growth rate of only 1%, and that
is before stripping out all the enhancements to the house.

The White House is a good example, however, of the problem
of comparing house prices over time because the White House of
today is quite a bit different from the house that Hoban built. It has
undergone several expensive enhancements beyond the bunker
and the rather substantial extensions, including a bowling alley,
a putting green and, most recently, a basketball court.*

This long-term example again shows how careful we have to
be in talking about nominal house price increases – we really do
have to convert our perceptions into a real measure of annual
returns. Of course, the White House is no average house, but
across the US there has been a similar pattern.

## FINANCIAL CRISES AND HOUSE PRICE VOLATILITY

In a sense, the US is the home of financial crises. The famous
Wall Street Crash of 1929 led to the worldwide Great Depression of the 1930s. And of course the US is also the epicentre of
the biggest global downturn since then: the Great Recession. The
subprime crisis that began in the US housing market in 2007 later
spread around the world, resulting in the severe recession that
has brought down some of the world's largest financial institutions, cost millions of people their jobs, and even threatened the
solvency of national governments. Both these crises, and others
in between, have been intertwined with the average US home –
in both their effects *and* their causes.

For Americans, the dream of owning your own home is almost
as old as the dream of freedom and democracy. For the first

*To get a fair comparison requires adjusting for the upgrades via the hedonic
method, or, if using matched pairs (looking at how much the same house sells
for over time), the White House would certainly need to be excluded for not
being comparable over time.

settlers, only those who owned property could vote, while their tenants were considered only temporary citizens and had fewer rights – and something in the connection between the two has stuck.[2] The US has a high level of home ownership, and the recent housing boom has shown that many people who did not own their home shared that dream. America too, it seems, has a love affair with houses – but, as we will see, there has been plenty of heartache.

## ONE HUNDRED AND TWENTY YEARS OF HOUSE PRICES

To get a sense of US house prices it would be useful to see how they have changed over the tumultuous events of the last hundred years. Unlike in the UK, many researchers have looked extensively at this question, none more so than the Yale economist Professor Robert Shiller, who put together an index of US house prices stretching back to 1890 for the second edition of his bestselling book *Irrational Exuberance*.[3]

Robert Shiller's house price index runs from 1890 to 2010 and was constructed by joining together several different series, all of which varied in methodology and quality. The index for 1890–1934 is based on the repeat sale price of a given house,[4] thus providing a closer like-for-like comparison than the data for 1934–53, which is based on median house prices.[5] For the years 1953–75 the data comes from the Bureau of Labor Statistics – specifically, the home purchase component of the consumer prices index. The data does control for quality change by holding the age and size of homes constant. From 1975 onwards all the data comes from repeat-sales indices, with the 1975–87 period using the Office of Housing Enterprise Oversight (OFHEO) series and the 1987–2010 period using the Case–Shiller series.

## THE EMERGENCE OF THE UNITED STATES (1890–1914)

When General Robert E. Lee surrendered his Army of Northern Virginia on 9 April 1865, marking the end of the Civil War, the newly reunited states of America took a huge stride towards establishing themselves as a global power.[6] America had plentiful land brimming with natural resources, labour arriving from all over the world and free-moving capital that, together with the newly found peace, set a firm foundation for growth. Industrialization was able to spread across the continent at the speed of the ever-expanding railway.*

Yet looking at Shiller's index, it is clear that house prices were not galloping ahead in either nominal or real terms after 1890. With inflationary pressures managed via the gold standard, house prices were pretty much flat over the twenty-four-year period shown in figure 2.1.†

House prices did fluctuate by around ±20% in real terms. Broadly, these swings followed the business and financial cycles, but advances and declines were relatively short-lived and prices reverted back to their norm.

We can see the influence of the rapid economic growth of the early 1890s, followed by a period of stagnation as the economy fell back between 1892 and 1896. By 1893 the railway companies had overexpanded with weak balance sheets and, starting with the Philadelphia and Reading Railroad Company, began to collapse. As these companies failed, they brought down some banks that had either lent too much money to them or speculated in their stock. Confidence was badly bruised and the episode became known as the Panic of 1893. At the time it was the worst depression America had ever experienced: unemployment rose to over 15% and house prices were brought back to their previous levels.

The economy rebounded strongly in the decade after 1897, with real GDP rising by two-thirds and real GDP per capita rising

*Railways grew rapidly from around 9,000 miles of track in 1850 to 50,000 miles by 1870 and 130,000 miles by 1890. This enabled substantial efficiency gains in agriculture and a large industrial and consumer market.

†Under the gold standard each currency was worth a fixed quantity of gold (or sometimes silver). The money supply, therefore, only increased as more gold was discovered, and gold reserves grew very slowly. With a relatively fixed amount of money, inflation was typically only found when a product was scarce, driving up its price. General inflation of the type we see today is very much a post-Second World War phenomenon.

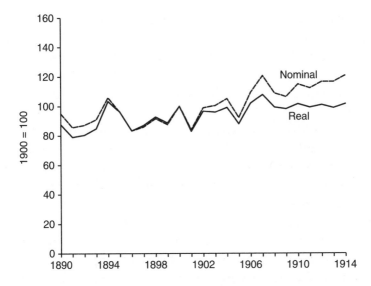

**Figure 2.1.**  US real house price index, 1890–1914.
*Data sources*: Shiller; Measuring Worth.[7]

by over 30% over the decade. But this strong economic growth seems to have had little effect on real house prices. Quite differently from our recent experience in the UK, house prices did not increase, despite huge population growth, growth in GDP per capita, rising earnings, low inflation and stable interest rates.

The next upswing in house prices came between 1905 and 1907, only to fall back again by 1910. This was the period either side of the Panic of 1907.[8] The economy had been growing strongly through 1905–6, and then a combination of factors (mainly the San Francisco earthquake and a rise in international interest rates) caused the economy to slow and the stock market to start to fall. With the economy and stock markets faltering, a stock market panic started when speculators failed to corner the market in the United Copper Company. The financing for this attempt came from the intriguingly named Knickerbocker Trust Company, one of the largest of a new breed of investment companies that invested in shares, including each other's shares, and which again had weak balance sheets – balance sheets that started to unravel as this attempt to rig the market failed. In a story we will recognize today, as one company or bank failed it dragged down others; and as they went bust, investors tried to cut their losses and sell their remaining stock, which in turn caused more failures, panics and falls.

This vicious cycle was halted when John Pierpont (J.P.) Morgan and other bankers stepped in to provide liquidity and support the market. Nowadays, we expect the central bank to do this, but the US had no central bank at this time and it was therefore left to individual banks to try and calm the markets. Unsurprisingly, the Panic of 1907 provided the impetus for the Federal Reserve Act of 1913, which set up much of the banking regulation that we see today and facilitated the later use of market support mechanisms.

During the downswing of this cycle, house prices fell by around 15%. What is most striking about this period, however, is that with gains being cancelled out by falls, house prices in 1914 were about the same as, if not slightly lower than, prices had been twenty-five years earlier. The market gyrations had been driven mostly by the business cycle, heightened by the two main financial crises of the times – the Panics of 1893 and 1907. The huge growths in population, output and incomes seem to have had no lasting effect on real house prices.

## THE FOUNDATIONS OF THE MODERN HOUSING MARKET

### *War, Pandemics, Bubbles and Recessions (1914–33)*

Between 1914 and 1921 real house prices dropped by a third. For the first time in this data series we see a divergence between the growth in nominal prices for houses and the fall in real prices. Although the US did not enter the First World War in 1914, it did experience the initial recession that the war caused, followed by the rapid inflation of the war years. By the time the US entered the war in 1917, as we can see in figure 2.2, house prices had already started to decline, and the decline accelerated after that. At least

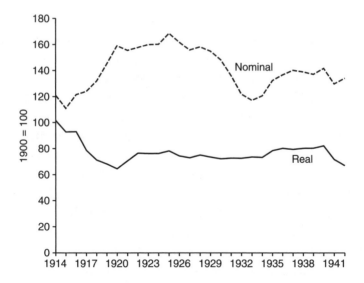

**Figure 2.2.** US real house price index, 1914–42.
*Data sources*: Shiller; Measuring Worth.

as important as the war's effect on house prices was the influenza
pandemic of 1918–19 (which infected 28% of Americans and killed
675,000).

America suffered three brief but significant recessions in the
years following the war. Immediately at the end of the war, the
shift from wartime production and the demobilization of millions
of troops, combined with weak international demand, caused a
short but sharp recession. Just a few months later, the depression
of 1920–21 hit production and employment and a mild recession
occurred in 1923–24.

But out of this came a period of unprecedented growth
economically and culturally: the Roaring Twenties. Fuelled by
advances in technology, transport, communication and infrastructure, company earnings more than quadrupled from 1921
to 1926. But despite the twenties roaring by outside their win-
dows, we can see that real house prices were merely whimpering
in both nominal and real terms.

Then, in October 1929, disaster struck: stock prices on Wall Street fell by a staggering 13% in a single day soon known as 'Black Tuesday'. From 1929 to 1932 the stock market shed 80% of its value and over the following decade unemployment in the US rose to one-in-four. Unlike today the government played a limited role in stimulating the economy, and many argue its policies ushered in a period of unprecedented deflation and economic misery.

When the economy nosedived, mortgage providers simply refused to lend or refinance. In 1932 and 1933 there were over half a million foreclosures and by mid 1933, over a thousand mortgages were being foreclosed on every day.[9] Even back then, about two-fifths of Americans owned their own homes and so the effects were widespread and, passed down through books such as *The Grapes of Wrath* by John Steinbeck, the story resonates with us today. Indeed, many would argue that the Great Depression was the formative experience for the modern US – a nightmare it does not want to repeat – and, even eighty years on, that it forms the most important narrative in the American subconscious as policymakers address current economic issues.

Despite the economic and personal devastation, we can see that house prices remained broadly flat in real terms over the period. This is because while nominal house prices fell by 30%, the price of other goods fell by even more, with the result that real house prices held up. We will see this pattern – where house prices are a good store of real value in highly deflationary periods – again in other countries. So, as stocks were crashing and prices with them, those who owned their houses outright retained the wealth tied up in their house through these difficult times.

However, even if they had realized it at the time, this would have been of little comfort to those who had borrowed and were having to pay interest on houses that were falling in nominal terms. This historical example illustrates the flip side of borrowing to finance your home: while in periods of rising prices it multiplies your returns, in periods of falling prices (even when real prices hold up) you can be left in a debt trap, with a large mortgage secured against a house that has dropped in value.* It was the suffering that was endured by the millions who lost their homes that led to the redefining of the role of the state in the housing market.

### The New Deal for Home Ownership (1933–42)

In 1933, Franklin D. Roosevelt's government established new federal agencies with the aim of reinvigorating a depressed US economy. One of the most significant of these changes was to radically improve the opportunities for ordinary Americans to own their own homes.

The Federal Home Loan Bank Board that had already been established in 1932 was now mandated to encourage and oversee local mortgage associations, called savings and loans associations (S&Ls). Similar to British building societies, S&Ls would take in deposits and lend to local homebuyers. Roosevelt also introduced insurance on these deposits to guard against the fear of bank failures, which had plagued the previous few years. On top of this, the Federal Housing Administration was to guarantee these mortgages, allowing the S&Ls to promote loans that were large (up to 80% of the purchase price), long (twenty years or more) and that had low, fixed interest.

The introduction of the Federal Housing Administration helped standardize the mortgage market, paving the way for other lenders from out of town to support the local mortgage associations through a secondary market. In 1938, the Federal National Mortgage Association – nicknamed Fannie Mae – was authorized to issue bonds and use the proceeds to lend to the S&Ls.

With the US government owning Fannie Mae, insuring deposits in the S&Ls and – through the Federal Housing Administration – guaranteeing long-term mortgages, it was effectively

---

*The problem being that debt is in nominal terms and in deflationary periods prices and wages fall but the amount you owe stays the same, making it harder to repay. The real value of the debt rises as your income falls. This is the famous Fisher debt–deflation trap.

underwriting a large part of the US mortgage market. Citizens were actively encouraged to become homeowners. The modern US property-owning democracy, the backdrop of the American dream, was born.

Through this period, real house prices remained stable. Any rise was at best slight, but in the context of the times that was perhaps not so bad. America stayed out of the Second World War until Pearl Harbor brought it into the conflict. By 1942, real house prices were 30% below their 1914 level, but they had at least been stable in real terms for the previous precarious twenty years.

## THE POSTWAR BOOM BYPASSED HOUSE PRICES

### *The Return to Growth (1942–73)*

America was much more heavily involved in the Second World War than it had been in the First. This time, a quarter of American men went to war and US involvement changed America's standing and role in the world. With demand booming before and after the war, unemployment fell and output and real wages rose.

It was not just the return to peace and prosperity when the war ended that led to the dramatic rise in prices. The Servicemen's Readjustment Act of 1944, also known as the GI Bill, among other benefits provided subsidies for war veterans to buy houses, helping seventeen million people to buy property. The high postwar birth rate coupled with advances in medicine also shifted population growth up a gear. In the following two decades, seventy-six million children were born in the US. This would change the shape of American society: the baby boomers had arrived, bringing with them a greater demand for housing. The government support for home ownership, established in the New Deal, was now being put into action. However, while real house prices rose rapidly between 1942 and 1947, they then dropped back to their old pre-First World War levels, and there they remained for many years.

**Figure 2.3.** US real house price index, 1942–95.
*Data sources*: Shiller; Measuring Worth.

Even if real house prices were not showing much movement, we all know that this was a period of remarkable progress. There were mild recessions but they were aberrations on a path of scientific and industrial progress, with an ever-increasing number of people enjoying greater wealth than ever before. As the Civil Rights movement gained momentum, the S&Ls broadened their lending to ethnic minorities. Again the government intervened. It put in place two more props beneath the housing market: Fannie Mae's operations were split into its *explicitly* government-supported lending, which became the Government National Mortgage Association (known as Ginnie Mae), and a private lending corporation, which kept the name Fannie Mae. To increase the number of loans available even further, a second private company was set up: the Federal Home Loan Mortgage Corporation (Freddie Mac).

Yet despite all this government support, and with home ownership increasing, reaching 64% in 1973, real house prices remained unmoved, as can be seen in figure 2.3.

## Oil Shocks and Adjusting to Inflation (1973–80)

The oil shocks of 1973, when OPEC quadrupled oil prices, and 1979, when the Iranian Revolution led to a doubling of oil prices, caused both a recession and high levels of inflation. In nominal terms house prices boomed, doubling between 1973 and 1980, but almost all of this increase was due to inflation. In real terms, house prices rose for a while before sliding back to their old levels.

The increase in real prices could perhaps be due to real interest rates being temporarily negative as inflation was rising, before reverting back to their normal real level,* or it could be that houses were a good asset to hold as inflation reduced the value of savings and other investments, or it could be that it takes us a while before our understanding of real price levels reasserts itself. Whatever the cause, real prices quickly reverted to their historical levels. For those families that stayed put it would have made little difference, but for those buying or selling, such a turbulent market would have contributed to large gains and losses.

## The Savings and Loans Crisis (1980–95)

Before the oil shock, the US had been making progress in broadening home ownership, in large part by using the savings and loans associations. But what started out as an embodiment of the American dream soon turned into a nightmare. By the end of the 1980s, S&Ls were to have a crisis all of their own.

By the early 1980s, the S&Ls were losing money fast. Inflation was eroding the value of houses and the money the S&Ls had lent people to purchase them. S&Ls found it difficult to raise the interest rates they charged their borrowers as many loans had been taken out with fixed interest rates or had other restrictions. Meanwhile, the S&Ls were having to pay higher interest rates

*If inflation is an unexpected surprise, then the level of interest rates may not take into account this inflation. For a period, until expectations of inflation correspond with actual inflation, real interest rates may be low or even negative.

themselves to borrow from other lenders. Something had to be done. It was felt by the Reagan administration that the cure was tax reliefs and deregulation.

Under the new legislation, S&Ls were permitted to invest in more than just mortgages, and they were given more freedom over setting their interest rates. The government provided even more support, increasing the insurance on deposits made with them to $100,000. Less responsible S&Ls now had money to play with: some of them invested their money in highly dubious schemes, others simply stole it. One crooked scheme, known as the 'flip', involved buying cheap land and then reselling that land at inflated prices to an accomplice whose funds came from an S&L mortgage that would never be repaid, with the co-conspirators pocketing the gain. 'The best way to rob a bank', recalled William Crawford, the Commissioner of the California Department of Savings and Loans, 'is to own one'.[10]

Like any Ponzi scheme, the bottom soon fell away. When the regulators were forced to move in, nearly five hundred S&Ls had to be shut down, bankrupting the government agency responsible for insuring depositors. More than a thousand white-collar felony convictions followed. The final cost of the S&L scandal was $153 billion (around 3% of GDP), and taxpayers were liable for $124 billion of that total.

Nationally, activity in the housing market ground to a halt along with the wider economy, leading to another recession in the early 1990s and to another fall in house prices, back to the average levels of the 1950s – and therefore to the same real level as in 1914.

### THE SECURITIZATION OF MORTGAGES:
### SETTING THE STAGE FOR THE GROWTH OF SUBPRIME

In the fallout from the S&L crisis there were millions of mortgage holders whose lenders were going bust. The S&Ls, even those that were above board, had overstretched themselves and were stuck with a lot of mortgages that no one else seemed to trust and which most regarded as junk. A clever new technique that would become synonymous with another crisis twenty years later came into play: securitization. In his book *Liar's Poker*,[11] Michael Lewis describes the birth of this market and, from his position as a trader at the investment bank, he observes how Salomon Brothers bought out many of the mortgage liabilities of the S&Ls at rock bottom prices and bundled them together before selling them on.*

This was a different world from the S&Ls of the previous fifty years, when the loans made by a bank were held on their books and the risk of any non-repayment therefore stayed squarely with the bank, making them (when they were operating properly) cautious about granting loans. But with mortgages bundled up and sold on, the stage was set for banks and others to earn their money by just originating mortgages as fast as they could, parcelling them up and selling them on. As well as passing on the income from the mortgage, they also passed on the risk of non-repayment. Considering that banks earned their fees by issuing mortgages, and were no longer reliant on repayment, perhaps it is unsurprising that lending standards dropped.

### THE GREAT BUBBLE (1995–?)

'We want everybody in America to own their own home', said George W. Bush in 2002. By 2003, Bush would go further with the American Dream Downpayment Act, which challenged lenders to create 5.5 million new homeowners – particularly targeting the

---

*Securitization involved each household's mortgage interest payment making up a small part of another 'securitized' bond. A bank could sell a thousand mortgages and then package these up in a bond and sell the income stream and the risk on to an investor, leaving them free to lend more. A more sophisticated version split this income stream into tranches, so that the first tranche had first rights to any income and the lowest tranche had the last rights. Since it was considered extremely unlikely that very many mortgages would fail, these higher tranches were usually considered a high-quality, low-risk investment. It would take twenty years for this assumption to be tested.

ethnic minorities, who were less likely to own their homes. The American Dream had a new lease of life.

Race had played a role in lending decisions for a long time – a practice called 'redlining' – and there was a focus on correcting this.* A key development was the Financial Institutions Reform, Recovery, and Enforcement Act of 1989, which critically changed the HDMA† data that lenders were required to disclose to the regulators (and to the public) to include the race and income of applicants for all loan applications and not just for approved loans. This data allowed denial rates to be compared across races and showed that, even when income was taken into account, ethnic minorities were significantly more likely to be denied mortgage credit. The data also allowed greater examination of the enforcement of existing legislation such as the Community Reinvestment Act. Perhaps partially because of these changes, during the recent housing boom the number of home purchase loans increased most dramatically in relative terms for the previously underserved minorities. According to HMDA data, between 1999 and 2005 mortgages to African Americans increased by a factor of 3.6, to Hispanics by a factor of 4.8, but for whites they only increased by a factor of 1.7.

Securitization brought with it the tools to issue more mortgages, opening the mortgage market up to people whose low

---

*There has been a long history of redlining in America, and its role was officially endorsed by the Federal Housing Administration in the 1930s.[12] Racial integration was discouraged, with the Federal Housing Administration's 1935 underwriting manual warning of the detrimental impact on a neighbourhood of the 'infiltration of inharmonious racial or nationality groups'. Several attempts were made to fight the practice, with Kennedy prohibiting it in 1962 for federal housing programmes, but it continued for many years, even if not explicitly. For example, a bank could have a policy of specifying a minimum loan size. While this is not explicitly racist, it had the known effect of ruling out the majority of black borrowers.

†The Home Mortgage Disclosure Act (HDMA) of 1975 required lenders to disclose certain data to check lenders were not discriminatory and were working in the interests of local communities. The 1989 Act extended disclosure requirements.

credit rating had previously been considered subprime – that is, below the normally acceptable levels. But with securitization, a bank could now sell such a mortgage bundled up with others, passing the risk on to others that were willing to take it. Towards the middle of the decade, most of the owned homes in America's poorest communities were funded by a subprime mortgage. At their peak, subprime mortgages accounted for about 20% of the market. The call for more homeowners was being heard: by the end of 2005, 69% of American families now owned rather than rented, compared with 64% ten years earlier.

Through the alchemy of finance, these subprime mortgages were eagerly financed by institutions from around the world. Between 1980 and 2007 the value of securitized debt put together in this way rose from $200 million to £4 trillion – over 25% of US GDP. By 2007, only twelve countries and ten companies world-wide were rated AAA, but at the peak of the market many thousands of securitized instruments were given this rating.*

House prices boomed as never before, as shown in figure 2.4, virtually doubling in real terms. Now housing really was a money-making machine. Prices were rising at 10% each year in nominal terms and at a staggering 7% in real terms. At a growth rate of 7% you can double your real wealth every ten years – and that is before leverage. It was an exciting and intoxicating time to own a property.

But one of the benefits of hindsight is that we know this golden age did not last. Real prices are down by more than 35% from their 2006 peak, and the decline does not yet show any signs of being reversed. We now know that this was another financially driven bubble – larger and more pervasive than the earlier bubbles we have explored, but equally unsustainable. It was certainly not a new paradigm.

---

*A rating of AAA is meant to mean that there is almost no risk of the bond defaulting. Standard & Poor's point out that after fifteen years only around 1% of AAA-rated corporate bonds have defaulted, against a figure of 8% for BBB-rated bonds and 57% for CCC.

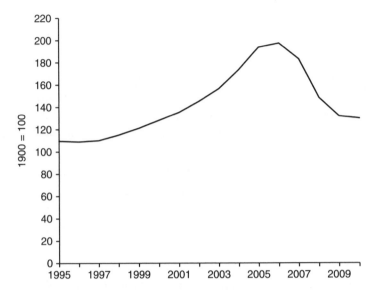

**Figure 2.4.** US real house price index, 1995–2010.
*Data sources*: Shiller; Measuring Worth.

In 2005, Robert Shiller's incisive book outlined each of the main reasons given during the boom years to explain why things were different this time. Some cited the growing population, and in particular the baby boomers, but population growth was not new and had not caused such swings before. Others claimed there was a shortage of land, but the 2000 census noted that only 2.6% of land in the US was urbanized – nor had land become that much more expensive.[13] Some experts argued there was a shortage of housing; but anyone visiting Florida now can wander around the empty houses that were built in a wave of unnecessary construction. Some suggested that the cost of building a house itself might have increased, but this was not the case. The benefit of the long data series, and of knowing how prices then collapsed, means we too can rule out these causes, despite the passion with which they were espoused during the boom.

One of the myths of the bubble, and its bursting, was that no one could have seen it coming – some did, and some investors made a fortune backing their beliefs with well-placed bets (most notably John Paulson's hedge fund, which made $20 billion[14]). It now seems clear that Shiller and others were right that this was a bubble, facilitated by low interest rates and a huge increase in credit via the mechanism of securitization. Some stopped seeing houses as homes and instead saw them purely as investments. According to the HMDA, about 15% of all homes purchased in 2004 were second homes used as investment properties or vacation homes. Many other homes were purchased by people who were really not in a financial position to take on house ownership – lured into the market by a mix of overenthusiastic, self-interested and, in some cases, dishonest financial institutions.*

The successful investor Sir John Templeton once said that 'the most dangerous words in investing are "this time it's different" '. By the end of 2010, house prices in the US were down 30% in nominal terms and 35% in real terms.† They are now at about the same real level that they were in 1894 and very close to the typical level we have seen through much of the period since 1890. It seems that this time was not so different after all, just rather more spectacular.

The broader costs of this bubble are still being felt today. The collapse of house prices, and the associated collapse in investments tied to house prices, has weakened the balance sheets of many banks. In some cases it has destroyed them. The US government, driven by fear of a return to the 1930s, has taken much of the impaired debt onto its balance sheet, causing public debt

---

*Around 80% of mortgages issued to subprime borrowers were adjustable-rate mortgages that began with low interest rates to tempt borrowers but quickly rose to market-level rates for the remainder of the mortgage's term. Borrowers who could not make these higher payments were forced to refinance their mortgage, something that became increasingly difficult as house prices fell. Interest rates eventually tightened and once the teaser rates expired, many households fell behind on their payments.

†Prices continued to fall into 2011. Prices fell 3% in the first quarter – the biggest quarterly fall since the collapse of Lehman Brothers.

to soar.* The collapse in subprime mortgages has caused a global financial crisis and the most severe recession since the 1930s.

The cost for individuals has been high. American owner–occupiers owed a sum equivalent to 99% of US GDP by the end of 2006, compared with just 38% fifty years earlier.[16] Foreclosure levels have tripled to around 1.5%. About 13% of all homes in the US have negative equity but 35% of those that bought in 2005 and 2007 are in negative equity and over 40% of those who bought in 2006. For many it will be years before they will overcome the losses from their foray into the housing market.

### LESSONS FROM AMERICA

So, what can we gauge from 120 years of US data? The first lesson is that, as in the UK, we need to look past nominal prices and focus on real, inflation-adjusted prices, and in order to control for the very long time periods involved we need to look at the compound average annual returns (see figure 2.5). The nominal price for a house rose more than thirty-five times over (by 3,560%) during the 120-year period, equating to an increase of around 3% per year. In real terms, house prices increased by 24% in total up to the end of 2010 – a much more modest growth rate of below 0.2% per year. Indeed, the first fifty years show a decline in house prices.

The most striking message from the real house price data (as is more clearly seen in figure 2.6) is that this tiny rate of below 0.2% growth is pretty close to flat – over 120 years. This is very different from the data that we saw for the UK, which showed prices rising well ahead of inflation since the 1950s. US property has produced much lower investment returns. Relative to an investment in US

*Depending on the definition used, US public debt now stands at between 60% and 90% of GDP, a level last seen during the Second World War. Economists Kenneth Rogoff and Carmen Reinhart, who have written an influential book looking at past crises, argue that levels above 90% have a negative impact on future growth rates.[15]

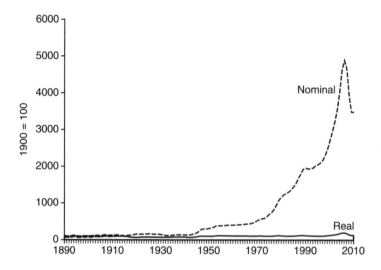

**Figure 2.5.** US house price index, real and nominal, 1890–2010.
*Data sources*: Shiller; Measuring Worth.

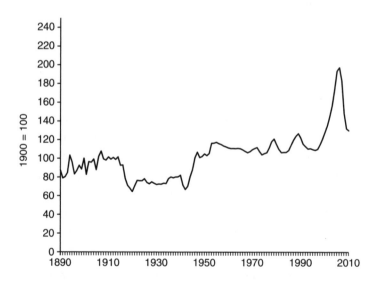

**Figure 2.6.** US real house price index, 1890–2010.
*Data sources*: Shiller; Measuring Worth.

stock markets, these returns have been very low.* This is not to argue that the decision to own a home has been a mistake – there are the benefits of not paying rent and there are some tax benefits that subsidize interest payments versus rent.† And of course there are all the non-financial benefits of owning a home as well. While some made fortunes during the upswings in the market, the last hundred or so years of data show that owning a house is not the wealth-creating machine that it is perceived to be in the UK.

The other thing we can see is that there are some very long cycles involved, and this means that house prices can linger at different levels for decades. For most of the period we have studied, house prices oscillated around the 1900 level, but the period between the start of the First World War and America's entry into the Second World War saw house prices stuck at only around 75% of this level. Weak demand, numerous recessions and a deflationary environment seemed to conspire to keep house prices below their average level. For those unlucky enough to buy their home just before this period, or lucky enough to buy just before it ended, the swing in real wealth would have been very substantial.

Putting these structural shifts in price levels to one side, we can see that there were numerous smaller cycles of typically ±20% throughout the period. Often these were driven by the business cycle, or by inflationary or deflationary environments. Most of the time, however, they seem to have been driven by booms in the financial markets and the availability of credit, in all cases followed shortly afterwards by a reversing of the expansion. We can also see, perhaps more clearly in the US than anywhere else, these cycles occurring quite rapidly. The market systems combined with

---

*Real US stock market returns with reinvested dividends have been between 6% and 7% not only for the last hundred years but also for the period since 1820.

†Since the first federal income tax was introduced in 1913, mortgage interest payments have been tax deductible. It is a scheme that costs the US taxpayer upwards of $70 billion in forgone revenue every year. Attempts to abolish it were overruled by President Reagan, who was unequivocal in his objection. It was, he said, 'part of the American dream'.

the fact that mortgages are typically non-recourse makes adjustments happen quite rapidly relative to other countries.*

For all the short-term risks and opportunities that these cycles create, however, we come back to the fact that houses have only just kept ahead of inflation. This is despite the huge growth in population, the size of the economy, the average level of income, supportive government policies and over a century of financial innovation. This goes against the beliefs that many of us hold in the UK. The experience of the US simply does not fit with the theory that house prices increase well ahead of inflation because of growth in earnings, population and the like. Clearly we need to keep looking. Our next step is a country from which many US immigrants came: Norway.

---

*Many mortgages in the US are non-recourse, meaning that if you cannot pay back your mortgage you can give the house to the lender and the lender has no further ability to take any other assets you own or to force you to pay interest for years to come. In most other countries you would still be liable for the mortgage loan even if you were to send the keys back to the bank. One consequence of non-recourse mortgages is that losses on real estate can affect banks far more quickly. When house prices fall in the US, more people leave their homes to the banks, forcing the banks to sell the house in a hurry and at an even lower price to minimize their loss, driving house prices down yet further. As a result, the US market generally has quicker falls in house prices than elsewhere.

# CHAPTER 3

# ROUGH SEAS IN NORWAY

## ONE HUNDRED AND NINETY YEARS OF HOUSE PRICES

For Norway we can go even further back into history to explore how house prices have behaved. If you visit prosperous Norway today, and read in your guidebook about its agricultural economy of two hundred years ago, you may well view the country as a model of economic development. In 1819 its one million people mainly spent their time farming the land or fishing the seas. Yet over the following 190 years the population grew to around two million by 1900 and has now grown to nearly five million. In some ways it is still a quiet and humble country, but over the period in question it has industrialized and emerged as one of the richest countries in the world, in large part thanks to its discovery of oil in the 1970s.[1] But as we will see, its journey to become so successful has not been smooth sailing.

So far in this book we have seen two quite different stories from the UK and the US. In the UK there has been more or less steady growth in house prices over the last sixty years, particularly in the last fifteen or so. In the US there have been long periods of rising prices over the last hundred years, but these have been balanced by times when prices have retreated, so that over the twentieth century as a whole house prices barely rose in real terms. We continue our journey to find patterns and clues by looking at the market in Norway over the last two centuries.

We are fortunate that the Norwegian economists Øyvind Eitrheim and Solveig Erlandsen, bemoaning the lack of historical data on Norwegian house prices going back any further than 1980, have been motivated to construct an index that covers nearly two hundred years of prices in four Norwegian cities: Oslo, Bergen, Trondheim and Kristiansand.*

For each individual city they use data from property registers to compare how much the *same* house is sold for over time. This is known as the 'repeated sales' method, which is generally more accurate in understanding how the prices of existing houses change than the hedonic method that we saw used in the UK. To compare prices across Norway, Eitrheim and Erlandsen use the hedonic method to factor in the difference between locations.

### THE EPIC HISTORY OF NORWEGIAN HOUSE PRICES (1819–2010)

This long data series gives us the chance to examine house price levels throughout Norway's development and its inevitable ups and downs along the way. Figure 3.1 shows the index for house prices in pre-inflation, nominal terms and also in post-inflation, real terms (with 1900 = 100 in both cases). What strikes you at first is the enormous difference that including inflation makes to the size of increase in house prices. In nominal terms prices

---

*From 1897 they have data for all four cities and therefore a large number of observations. Before that the data set is somewhat smaller: only Bergen's records are available at the start of the period, in 1819, with the record for Oslo starting in 1841, that for Kristiansand in 1867, and that for Trondheim in 1897. This means that there are often fewer than fifty data points before about 1870, whereas there are well over a hundred per year from then on. It may therefore be the case that the nineteenth-century data needs to be taken with a little more caution than later observations.

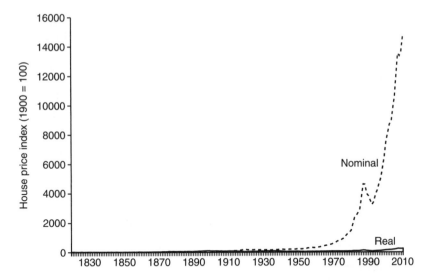

**Figure 3.1.** Norwegian house prices between 1820 and 2010, before and after inflation.

*Data sources*: Norges Bank; Statistics Norway.[2]

quadrupled between 1819 and 1900 and then increased 150-fold between 1900 and 2010.

We can appreciate the power of compounding when we consider that this 150-fold increase over 190 years is the result of a far less remarkable average growth rate of 4.6% per year. However, with inflation taken out we can barely see the real price snaking along the foot of the graph. The real increase in house prices has been a sixfold increase between 1819 and 1900 and a two-and-a-half-fold increase between 1900 and 2010, as shown in figure 3.2.

In the first few decades (1820–50), real house prices were quite volatile, but as a trend they did gently rise by around 1% per year. After that, there appears to be a rapid rise in prices over the rest of the nineteenth century (1850–1900), with house prices growing each year by an average of 2.7%. For most of the twentieth century (1900–1995) we can see that prices were much more volatile, but in spite of all this the real value of a house in 1995 was about

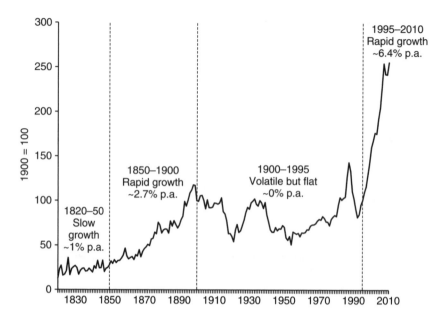

**Figure 3.2.** Real house prices in Norway, 1820–2010.
*Data sources*: Norges Bank; Statistics Norway.

the same as it was in 1900. This fact is very hard for most of us to incorporate into our beliefs about how house prices behave. Equally dramatic is the amazing boom in house prices in the last few years, with a remarkable annual growth rate of 6.4% between 1995 and 2010.

## THE NINETEENTH-CENTURY RECOVERY

In 1819, Norway was, like much of Europe at that time, still recovering from the Napoleonic Wars. It had just emerged from a three-hundred-year union with Denmark, and had been on the losing side in the Napoleonic Wars. Although ceded to Sweden, Norway operated independently under a broadly democratic constitution until it became fully independent in 1905.

The Napoleonic wars had seen rapid inflation, and as those wars ended in 1815 Norway entered a period of significant deflation. Not only did prices fall, but wages fell too, sometimes even faster than prices fell, which led to a fall in *real* (inflation-adjusted) wages. In other words, people were getting poorer. Indeed, it was not until the mid 1820s that standards of living returned to the levels that had been enjoyed in the late 1700s, and even then real wage growth was slow: between 1797 and the early 1860s real wages grew by barely 0.2% each year. Between 1820 and 1850 nominal house prices bobbled along without much change, but because of this deflation in general price levels, real house prices actually rose by an average of 1% each year. As we saw in the US, house prices can be a good store of real value in deflationary times.

Moreover, crises happening in other countries in Europe meant that demand for Norway's exports fell. In 1847 the British financial markets collapsed as the railway boom of the 1840s came to an end, and in 1848 the French began to revolt after a bad harvest and a financial crisis. Then came the effects of the Crimean War and the Panic of 1857, when the slowdown in world trade and the financial panic caused in the US by the failure of the Ohio Life Insurance and Trust Company combined to hit the Norwegian economy again. As Norway's currency was fixed at a standard quantity of gold (due to being on the gold standard), the country could not adjust its exchange rates and these international shocks were transmitted directly to the economy. This series of problems in the UK, France, the Crimea and the US caused the economy to slow and exports to fall, which in turn led to the failure of several companies.

Perhaps in part because of the low prices of the previous forty years, house prices began to rise rapidly in the last third of the nineteenth century, with most of the rise taking place in Oslo. At the start of the century, Bergen rather than Oslo was the largest city in Norway and was the commercial centre of the country. But this was soon to change. Oslo's population rose fourteenfold between 1815 and 1890, whereas in the same period Bergen merely

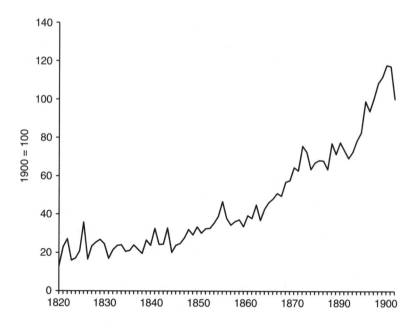

**Figure 3.3.** Real house prices in Norway, 1820–1900.
*Data sources*: Norges Bank; Statistics Norway.

tripled in size. The bulk of this growth occurred in the second half of the nineteenth century, which saw a huge influx of people into Oslo as the city enjoyed several advantages: industrialization was taking off, railroad expansion was centred on the city, its port was becoming the largest and most sophisticated in Norway, and the emerging financial and services sectors were clustering in the city.

This population increase was associated with growth in the economy as the country became a major exporter of timber, fish and shipping services. This economic resurgence led to a rise in real wages, which increased at a real rate of 1.7% per year between the early 1860s and 1899, compared with the anemic 0.2% annual growth of the previous sixty years. And for a change the external environment was positive, with the international boom that followed the ending of the Franco-Prussian War, which heralded a period of rapid growth in international trade.

We can see the positive effect on house prices in figure 3.3, with house prices doubling in real terms from the mid 1860s through to the mid 1870s.

But, by the late 1870s, house prices and incomes were growing out of control and the brakes needed to be applied. Interest rates rose and the money supply shrunk. The resulting deflation also lowered house prices, making debts more burdensome and forcing several businesses to go bust. As the economy stalled, emigration soared, in particular to the US, with around 250,000 people emigrating between 1879 and 1893 at a time when Norway's population was only around two million. Only Ireland sent more of its people across the Atlantic, and they did so over a longer period of time. As a result, house prices stagnated and fell back slightly in real terms.

After the nadir was reached around 1886, however, the economic cycle swung back up again. A boom in the 1890s saw growth across the board in manufacturing, banking and construction. The fundamentals of booming economic conditions and a return to population growth soon led to a surge in housing demand and, with supply fixed in the short term, a surge in prices too. This spurred the builders into action. They set about constructing swarms of four- and five-storey brick apartment blocks for rent in Oslo's inner city, most of which survive to this day. The number of new real estate companies in Oslo ballooned from sixteen in 1897 to forty-seven in 1898 and fifty-two in 1899. Once again, the money supply was loosened and interest rates fell, adding further finance to fuel speculation. Numerous new banks were started with new capital, helping to provide even more loans. The government also played a role by resuming work on the railways, which helped make Oslo a more attractive location for business.

By 1899 the property market looked quite different from the subdued market of the first half of the century. If you had bought in 1884 you would have doubled your money, in real terms, by 1899 – a period of only fifteen years. If you had bought in 1860 you would have tripled your money. But, as we will see, the boom prices of 1899 would not be seen again for nearly a century.

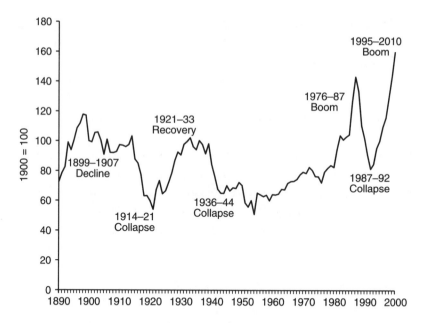

**Figure 3.4.**  Real house prices in Norway, 1900–1995.
*Data sources*: Norges Bank; Statistics Norway.


## THE VOLATILE TWENTIETH CENTURY (1899–1995)

Imagine that you were living in Oslo at the end of the nineteenth century. If you had been, you may very well have held similar beliefs about investing in housing as we now hold in the UK, but the next hundred years would give plenty of reasons to question those beliefs as house prices rose and fell wildly (see figure 3.4).


### *The Bursting of the 1899 Bubble*

As we have seen, by 1899 the Norwegian economy was firing on all cylinders, supported by increasingly overextended banks and low interest rates. But in June of that year a major pulp wood processor called General Consul Chr. Christophersen went bankrupt and its lenders had to write off most of their loans, resulting in significant losses.[3] Discontobanken, a major bank, was effectively insolvent and required support from the central bank. Other banks soon followed. The ensuing credit crunch ushered in a major recession, which was then made worse by a downturn in the world economy in 1901.

The result was a further lowering of demand for housing and the return of significant emigration. In 1905, one in every ten homes was vacant and a typical house was worth 75% of what it had sold for in 1899. Rents, meanwhile, were also down by around a quarter. The twentieth century had started with volatile house prices and things would only get wilder.

### The Collapse of 1914–21

At the outbreak of the First World War, Norway's neutrality meant it could trade with both sides, although the government was clearly supportive of the British and their allies. Unprecedented growth in household consumption followed. Yet when Germany started to target vessels that were supporting the Allies, it torpedoed many Norwegian ships and the economy soon headed in the same direction as those unlucky vessels. The postwar recession of 1920–21 also hit Norwegian exports, further damaging the battered economy.

Surprisingly, house prices during this period actually rose by over 50% in nominal terms. However, because of the very rapid inflation that occurred during the war, facilitated by Norway leaving the gold standard in 1914, prices in the rest of the economy rose by even more, so *real* house prices actually fell by about half.

### The Postwar Recovery 1921–33

The recovery in house prices after 1921 was in many ways the mirror image of the earlier fall. In nominal terms house prices were flat over the period, but because general price levels fell substantially (by around half), real prices actually rose (nearly doubling). In these two periods, as general prices in the economy soared or collapsed, house prices moved much less dramatically, and in that sense houses were a safe investment. If you needed to buy or sell, timing was important, but if you were a homeowner staying put, then you could watch the swings in price levels with at least some equanimity.

The deflation in prices was due to the government's attempt to restore the par value of the krone under the gold standard. The government's deflationary policies hit businesses and employment hard through the 1920s, but it may be that the enforced shake-out of firms and industries made them more efficient, possibly explaining why Norway was less badly affected by the 1930s depression.

### The 1936–44 Collapse

In the run-up to the Second World War inflation set in again, causing real house prices (but not nominal ones) to begin falling. While Norway once more remained neutral during the war, it was attacked and occupied by Nazi forces from 1940. Activity in the housing market slumped, and real prices fell further. This may not be particularly surprising but what is, perhaps, is that house prices did not bounce back after the war.

During the war, a number of new regulations to control prices for rented and owned houses were introduced. After the war, the left-leaning government embarked on a set of social democratic policies with a larger role for the state and more central planning. As part of this approach they retained the laws that had kept a lid on house prices, including higher taxes and controls on mortgage interest rates.

The house price index shows that the price freezes served their purpose. Nominal prices increased by a mere 15% from 1940 to 1954, a rise of just 1% each year, while inflation rose by 90% over the same period: a rise of 5% per year. The result was a drop in *real* house prices of around 40%.

The housing market was slowly liberalized between 1954 and 1969 at which point house prices ceased to be regulated. Having fallen to a postwar low in 1954, house prices increased by over half by 1970. Despite the freeing up of the market, however, houses were still cheaper in real terms than they had been at the beginning of the century and in the 1930s.

## The Oil Boom (and Bust) 1976–92

After two debilitating world wars, the country's luck changed. In 1969, the company Philips Petroleum discovered oil off the Norwegian coast. This meant that Norway was cushioned from the fall in living standards experienced by many other economies during the oil price shocks of the 1970s. In fact, as a seller of oil, Norway benefited hugely, with its oil revenues helping the country to become one of the world's richest economies, with per capita income still among the highest in the world today. It also meant that both the economy and house prices enjoyed a much smoother ride than they did in most other developed economies.

By the early 1980s the inflation caused by higher oil prices had subsided, meaning that both real and nominal house prices were growing, as was the rest of the economy. As in much of the rest of the world, Norway's banking and credit markets were liberalized during the 1980s, making it much easier for people to take on more debt. This deregulation ushered in another lending boom. Between 1984 and 1986, total bank loans grew by nearly 50%.[4] The increase in available credit passed through to households, who again used this to bid up the price of houses. Spending by households, businesses and even the government soared. From 1980 to 1987, house prices rose 70% in real terms.

But the boom left Norway vulnerable. The sharp decline in the oil price in early 1986, coupled with high wage demands, began to cause the system to creak. International investors started to lose confidence in the Norwegian krone, forcing banks into difficulties with their foreign loans. Unlike the crises in 1899 and the 1920s, most Norwegians now owned their own homes and were heavily invested in them, so it was not only a case of the economy pulling down house prices but also of house prices pulling down the economy, decimating economic activity and causing a deep recession. In 1991, at the peak of the crisis, four of the country's largest banks were forced to seek government support. By 1992 real house prices had fallen by about a third from their 1988 level.

### The Current Boom (1992–2010)

Once more the decline in prices turned, and, as can be seen in figure 3.5, the period between 1992 and 2010 has seen another house price boom, with prices rising by 150% in less than twenty years. In the 190 years of data for Norway, a rise of this scale has never been seen before. The four previous booms have seen smaller increases: the 1870s boom a doubling; the 1890s boom a two-thirds increase; the interwar rebound a doubling after a halving; and the oil-led boom of the 1970s and 1980s a doubling. We have seen that all those booms were followed by corrections, some of which were more dramatic than others. Although the recent rises have slowed, the latest boom has not yet shown any signs of such a reversal.

Norway does have the advantage of benefiting from high oil prices, but with mortgage lending now at 70% of GDP, compared with 50% ten years ago, there are fears that the economy may be just as vulnerable now to a fall in house prices as it has been before. We will not know for some time whether house prices will fall, or whether they are at a new, stable, high level that after many years of slow growth, regulation and volatility is in fact sustainable. In the 1920s about half the population owned, with half renting, but now, encouraged by tax breaks, subsidized mortgages and strong housing returns, nearly 80% of people own or have a stake in the

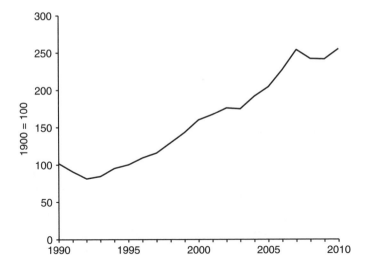

**Figure 3.5.** Real house prices in Norway, 1990–2010.
*Data sources*: Norges Bank; Statistics Norway.

homes in which they live. We can be sure that the future path for house prices will matter to many in Norway.

### LESSONS LEARNT FROM THIS NORSE SAGA

What lessons can we take away from this analysis of the history of Norwegian house prices? Across the whole period house prices have risen in real terms – by about 1.2% per year.[5] This is very dependent on the current high price levels, and on the prices from the nineteenth century being representative. If we just took the period from 1900 to 1995, as in figure 3.6, then house prices grew by almost exactly 0% annually, or 0.8% per year taking just the period from 1900 to 2010. So whether or not houses have been a good investment is open to interpretation.

Either way, the market has certainly been volatile. There have been decades during which prices have been flat or even falling (in real terms). There have been periods where inflation, deflation

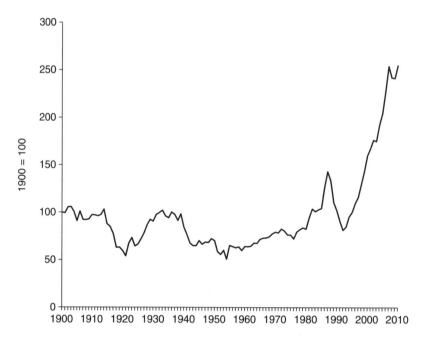

**Figure 3.6.** Real Norwegian house prices, 1900–2010.
*Data sources*: Norges Bank; Statistics Norway.

or government intervention has distorted the market. There have been periods where loose money and low interest rates have pushed up prices, only to be followed by a fall some years later.

Perhaps the most striking fact, however, is that the real house prices of 1900 were not seen again until the 1980s. Even if we ignore the deflationary and inflationary trough in the 1920s, and argue that prices were depressed by regulations in the 1940s and 1950s, it is hard to deny that an investment in housing over eighty years would have left you where you started. This is despite the Norwegian population growing from 2.2 million in 1900 to 4.1 million by 1980. So while we saw that the rapid population growth in Oslo in the nineteenth century affected house prices, population growth in general clearly has had little effect here on long-term house prices. During the same period, GDP rose more than twenty-five-fold and real wages tenfold. But this appears not to

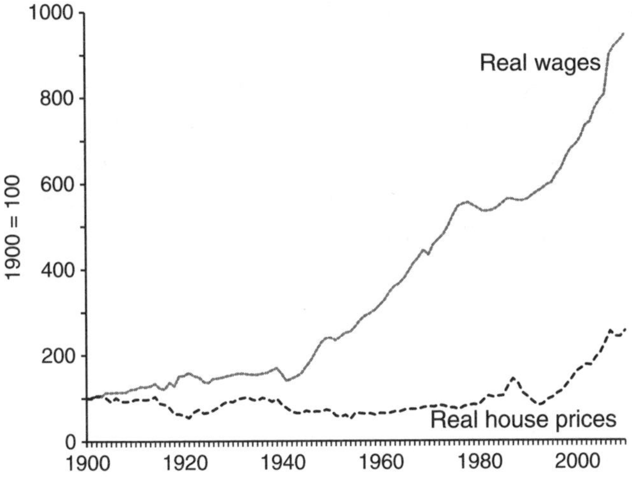

**Figure 3.7.** The poor relationship between real Norwegian house prices and real wages 1900–2010.

*Data sources*: Norges Bank; Statistics Norway.[6]

correlate with house prices either (see figure 3.7). This is perhaps the most surprising finding because many of us assume that house prices rise with earnings.

As we leave Norway, we can see that understanding the causes for past movements in house prices is difficult, let alone predicting them into the future. We can see that the strength of the economy, population changes, increases in earnings, interest rates and money supply, government tax policy and regulation, and construction all have an influence on house prices, particularly in the short and medium term. But the effect that each of these factors has on house prices is not consistent over time. Nor is it clear that they have much of an impact over the very long term, where house prices appear to have been stubbornly flat despite the huge changes that Norway has experienced over the last 190 years.

With Norway illustrating, more than once, that house prices can rise for a generation or more, it reminds us of the UK over the last few decades. But it equally shows that house prices can fall for a generation or more, which we have also seen in the US.

Over much of the twentieth century house prices have averaged the very low increases that we also saw in the US, and again this very modest progression of long-term house prices is at odds with our experience in the UK. Where Norway stands out over the last few years is that, unlike in the US, house prices show little sign of falling. As we turn south for the next stop on our journey, we will see that this is also the case elsewhere.

# CHAPTER 4

---

# UPS AND DOWNS DOWN UNDER

## NO SHORTAGE OF SPACE

WITH A LANDMASS AROUND 80% of the size of the US, Australia is the sixth-largest country in the world. With a population around 7% of that of the US, however, it is also one of the most sparsely populated. If Australia's population of twenty million were spread out evenly across the country, only three people would be left standing in each square kilometre, compared with 32 people in the US and 255 people in the UK. When you fly over Australia, the reason for this is pretty clear: the vast majority of the country is desert: the 'outback'.

To those whose first views of the continent were from ships arriving from Europe in the early nineteenth century, the sprawling, flat, arid landscape must have seemed unwelcoming. The only areas that colonists felt were worth inhabiting were the fertile coastal areas. The continent seemed to have little to offer – except as a place to send convicts. It would take events in another emerging country, the US, to set Australia off on the path to becoming the vibrant country that it is today – no longer viewed as a prison island but instead invariably ranked as one of the most desirable places to live in the world.

From 1848 to 1855, the US state of California was in a frenzy. Hundreds of thousands of people were racing there from all over the world in search of a glittering metal that might change their fortunes: the Gold Rush was in full swing. Among the countless numbers that arrived in 1849 – 'the 49ers' – one prospector named Edward Hargreaves noticed some odd similarities between the geology there and that back home on the east coast of Australia. Hargreaves returned empty handed, but the idea stuck with him and in 1851 he began exploring the waterholes not far from the city of Sydney. To his good fortune, and that of his country, this time he struck gold.

The next forty years were extremely prosperous for both Hargreaves and the fledgling nation. Backed up by a further gold rush in the 1860s, with even more gold found around Melbourne to the south, and rapid growth in the wool industry, Australia's population ballooned from 400,000 to 3.8 million between 1850 and 1900.[1] The gold bullion that was shipped to London each year paid for a growing stock of imports. The goldfield towns sparked investment in new businesses and invigorated the market for local produce. Where the people and the gold flowed, the railways, tramways and telegraph lines soon followed. The economy was expanding and the country thriving. By the late 1850s, Australia had become a land of wealth and opportunity, with many of the 'diggers' buying up land and setting up home.

## CONSTRUCTING A HISTORY OF HOUSE PRICES

Once again we are fortunate that a number of academic researchers have unearthed data about historical prices. Most prominently, Nigel Stapledon of the University of New South Wales has constructed a history of house prices in Australia going back as far as 1880 by piecing together data from a number of different sources.[2] For the years before 1950 the data comes from looking at the asking prices for houses advertised for sale in Sydney and Melbourne. For 1950–70 prices come from property market reports from *The Sydney Morning Herald* and *The Melbourne Age*. Spliced into that data are more recent price series from various official bodies across major state capital cities.

Stapledon has also attempted to adjust the data for the issue we have seen before – that houses change over time and can become non-comparable. He estimates that improvements to housing add around 0.95% per year to the value of the average house: this takes into account loft conversions, garage extensions, improved utilities and the like. He has also discovered that, as housing stock grows, the average house is getting further from the town centre. Stapledon estimates that this subtracts 0.35% per year from the value of the average house. So the net effect is that around 0.6% of the annual increase in house values is due to these two factors and the rest is due to prices rising on a like-for-like basis.

### AN OVERVIEW OF AUSTRALIAN HOUSE PRICES

Looking at the whole period, the data tell a story that will by now look familiar, albeit with some differences (see figure 4.1). In the period running up to 1900 we can see some of the cycles we have seen elsewhere. Between 1900 and the Second World War the index seems more robust than we have seen in other countries, but at the same time just as flat. From then until 1995 there is a rather jerky set of movements upwards, which need some explanation. In the last decade or so prices have rocketed to a new peak, at which they stand today. Just as in Norway, but unlike in the US, prices have not yet fallen.

Across the whole period from 1880 to 2010, house prices have risen at an annual real rate of 1.4%, but a large part of this rise has come in the last fifteen years. In the 115 years to 1995, prices rose more modestly at 0.9% per year, before jumping to an annual growth rate of 5.7% for 1995–2010. For most of the 130-year period houses were a solid, stable retainer of real value, but hardly a stellar investment. Given that, we should examine the long, steady part of the chart before turning to the more recent remarkable performance.

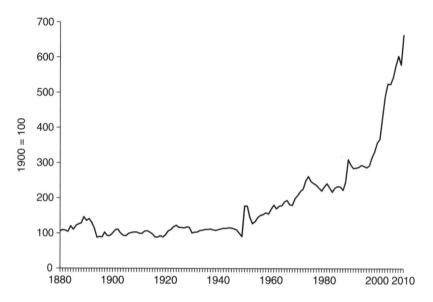

**Figure 4.1.** Real house prices in Australia, 1880–2010.
*Data source*: Stapledon.[3]

## NINETEENTH-CENTURY CYCLES (1880–1900)

As we saw in the US and in Norway, the late nineteenth century was the era of the archetypal business cycle. While the 1850s gold rush started near Sydney in New South Wales, it was most concentrated in the southern state of Victoria around the city of Melbourne. The Victorian authorities, eager to prevent their population from uprooting to join the gold rush in New South Wales, offered a reward of £200 for any gold found within two hundred miles of Melbourne. The incentive paid off. Within just six months of Hargreaves's find, gold was discovered in nearby Ballarat.[4]

In the ten years from 1881, Greater Melbourne's population grew by 70%, rising from just under 300,000 to just under 500,000. However, whilst the population rose by two-thirds, the number of houses built only increased by 50%. By today's standards, that amount of new house building is staggering, but back then it was simply not enough. The upward pressure on property prices was immense. Land prices on the outskirts of Melbourne rose by an average annual rate of 50% for much of the 1880s.[5] In some areas house prices were said to have doubled within just a few months.

While the boom had started because of a fundamental shift in demand for homes, speculation soon took hold. Lending to potential property owners was facilitated by so-called land banks, who, in addition to providing mortgages, also invested their own money in the land itself. Before long, these banks were effectively speculators themselves. Elsewhere, the buying bug was rife: in the stock market, in the mining companies and in property. By 1888 two-thirds of the new companies being incorporated in Australia were involved in property and financial activities.

As we have seen before, the cycle soon turned. Australia was rocked by the global recession and banking crisis that had gripped most of the industrialized world. As several Australian banks cut back their lending, some investors sensed danger – especially those who relied on rental income, which was not rising at the same pace as house prices. Prices started to fall, causing a number of bank runs and defaults. The vicious cycle that we have observed elsewhere set in and house prices crashed, giving up all of their previous gains.

Melbourne had been the main beneficiary of the boom period, with real house prices rising more than 60% between 1880 and their peak in 1889. Yet just as Melbourne experienced the best of the highs it also saw the worst of the lows. In the 1880s, when the chances of discovering gold had dwindled, Melbourne's population growth slowed as immigration began to stutter. By the mid 1890s, the total population had actually fallen by 12% and so too had house prices – by a stunning 50%.

The builders and suppliers had taken it for granted that the population and the economy would continue to grow. When it did not, there were suddenly too many houses. This will not be the last time that we will see a lag in construction first keep a boom going and then exacerbate the crash when it eventually arrives. The song *Waltzing Matilda*, often referred to as Australia's unofficial national anthem, was written in 1895 as the crash hit. It narrates the story of a penniless 'swagman' wandering the Australian bush, which was a familiar site during the miserable poverty of the time. The wanderer is so desperate that he has to steal for food – a crime punishable by hanging. When he gets caught killing a sheep, rather than be taken and tried he commits suicide by jumping into a watering hole – and stays on to haunt the site. It was against this cheery backdrop that Australia welcomed the new century.

## A SLOW WALTZ THROUGH THE THIRTIES (1900–1940)

The striking thing about house prices in the lead up to the Second World War is how flat they were. Compared with the US or Norway they were the picture of stability, even during the Great Depression. Some argue that house prices did not fall as steeply in Australia in the 1930s as they did elsewhere because they could not. By the time of the Great Depression, house prices were still scarred from the 1890s crash. Others point to the fact that while real incomes fell between 1929 and 1931, they then started to recover and were reasonably steady through the second half of the 1930s.

Whatever the explanation, the heights of the housing market in southern Australia in 1895 were not reached again until 1950.

## AFTER THE SECOND WORLD WAR (1940–95)

One of the strange features of house price movements after the war was the huge jump in prices in 1950. During the war (in 1942), the government introduced controls on house prices and land, limiting the amount that a house could be sold for to no more than 110% of its 1940 value. This cap on prices bit as inflation rose during and after the war. The controls were not lifted until 1949, by which time prices generally had risen by more than 30%. Real house prices fell in the same period by over 20%, although the controls generated a wave of creative ways to circumvent their restrictions so official house prices may not fully reflect all of the cash that actually changed hands.

From the 1950s to the 1990s real house prices rose gently, barring a few blips in the 1970s and 1980s. Over the whole period from 1940 to 1995 prices rose in real terms at around 1.8% each year.

### NEW HEIGHTS (1995–2010)

From the mid 1990s, house prices in Australia began to head in the same direction and at the same speed as in other Western markets: up and fast. House prices across Australia have risen by around 240% in nominal terms, and 130% in real terms since 1995: an average yearly growth rate of around 6%. What is more, unlike other countries we have looked at, house prices are still rising.

Over 115 years to 1995 real house prices had risen annually by an average of 0.9%. From 1880, it took ninety years for the first doubling of Australian house prices to occur – an increase that was more than matched in just the last fifteen years. Unsurprisingly, many in Australia wonder if price rises will continue, or if this is a bubble that will soon burst, as has happened in the US.

We have seen before how predicting house price movements over short periods with any degree of accuracy is hard, if not impossible. Nevertheless, we should at least explore what arguments are posed in Australia today to explain what has happened. Four main arguments have emerged to explain the boom: that there is a shortage of property; that the economy is booming, driving up prices; that property is a good investment relative to other available options; and that a bubble has emerged.

## A SHORTAGE OF SPACE?

One explanation for rising prices that has been put forward by the Reserve Bank of Australia, among others, is that there is a shortage of housing supply in Australia. Despite being one of the most scarcely populated places on earth, this argument claims that Australia has an insufficient supply of housing because of government regulation and controls that restrict the supply of land for urban use. By 2008, the number of new houses being built each year was under 150,000, which is below estimates of underlying demand at about 170,000.[6]

We have seen elsewhere that supply can be slow to respond to demand, pushing up prices. But we have also seen that over the medium term huge population rises have not typically led to sustainable rises in house prices. Supply typically does adjust – if it did not, then the millions who have arrived in Australia over the centuries would still be homeless. Australia saw its population rise from 3.8 million in 1900 to over 17 million in 1990 without creating a squeeze on housing.* The key question hanging over this argument is how long such an undersupply can last.

If there is an imbalance between those who want to purchase, and have the funds to do so, and the number of houses available, then there are a number of ways that demand and supply can be brought back into balance. In the short term, rising prices ration the limited supply. But in the longer term, other routes can be taken: building more houses, people moving towns or countries, people choosing to rent, and so on. To buy into the market at these very high prices is a bet that supply and demand will not come back into balance in the longer term.

---

*While Australia's population did grow rapidly between 2000 and 2010 (by around 15%), it grew even more rapidly in almost every decade of the twentieth century, with the fastest growth rate being the 1950s, where it rose by over 25%.

## A SECOND GOLD RUSH?

Where the house price increases of the 1880s and 1890s share a similarity with current house price increases is that they all coincide with massive resource booms. In the nineteenth century it was gold and in the last fifteen years it has been a staggering array of minerals. Australia is now the world's leading producer of lead, bauxite, diamonds, rutile, zircon and tantalum, the second largest supplier of uranium, zinc and nickel, the third biggest provider of iron ore, lignite, silver, manganese and gold, and the fourth largest producer of black coal and copper.[7] This resource extravaganza has supercharged the economy and people's incomes and has drawn people towards the resource-rich areas.

There is no doubt that the booming economy has raised people's incomes and therefore their ability to fund larger mortgages, and pay more for housing. But will they need to continue paying more over the longer term? Elsewhere, very large long-term increases in wealth have not had the dramatic effect on house prices that we see in Australia today. Between 1995 and 2010 per capita GDP, measured in 2010 Australian dollars, did rise by around 40% from $39,900 to $57,500, and over that period real house prices more than doubled. But between 1900 and 1995 real per capita GDP increased more than fourfold, from $9,100 to $39,900, and, as we have seen, house prices only doubled over that period.*

## A BETTER INVESTMENT?

Nigel Stapledon, reflecting on the market boom, argues that while income is important, there is no reason in theory why house prices should have a stable correlation with income, particularly if you

---

*This is not to argue that house prices do not go up with incomes, but there is an important difference between the logic that existing house prices go up in proportion to incomes and the alternative: that as our incomes rise, we invest more in newer and better properties and these are worth more.

view property as an investment.[8] His approach suggests a relationship between two other factors: the rental yield (the rent that can be earned as a percentage of the value of the house) and interest rates. An investor has two choices: invest in housing with a rental yield or invest in bonds (or other assets) with an interest rate yield. This argument suggests that low returns on other assets may drive property prices up, as investors buy property in search of better returns. This investment-driven approach could move prices in a different direction from that of average incomes.

Since the 1980s, house prices have moved ahead more quickly than rents have, meaning that yields have fallen. But, argues Stapledon, so have real interest rates. If the suggestion that prices might fall by 50% or so were realized, rental yields would move back up to the levels of the mid 1980s, when real interest rates were significantly higher (unless rents fall substantially). According to this argument, as long as real interest rates remain low, a crash in house prices is unlikely because investors do not have better places to put their money. Others argue that property yields, indeed possibly all yields, are very low from a historical perspective and that they need to be higher to reflect the risk inherent in investing in property. They argue that investors will eventually be unwilling to hold property at the current yields and it is this that will cause house prices to fall. We will have to wait until interest rates turn to see which argument is correct.

## AN AUSTRALIAN BUBBLE?

The other main argument that is proposed is that the house price rises represent a bubble. Those with this view have been hinting that prices in Australia might fall by magnitudes similar to the falls seen in the US. A 2010 article in *The Economist*, for example, compares house prices with earnings and estimates that Australian house prices may be overvalued by as much as 62%.[9]

Morgan Stanley economist Gerard Minack[10] argues that the key factor driving demand has been the dramatic rise in household borrowing. The decline in interest rates has helped consumers build a mountain of debt, as well as keeping rental yields down.

Professor Steve Keen of the University of West Sydney started publishing a monthly report in 2006 called *Debtwatch* to emphasize the dangers of rising private debt.[11] He believes that Australian house prices are a bigger bubble than existed in the US. As well as the increase in debt he points to the subsidies that the government has offered to first-time buyers under the First Home Owner Scheme, which provided up to A$21,000 towards the purchase of a first home. Looking at all the normal metrics of affordability, mortgage debt levels and the like, he expects prices to fall back significantly when the market turns, and he likens the market to a Ponzi scheme that will eventually collapse.

A fall in house prices of around 2% has been seen in the first quarter of 2011, and some forecasters see this as the potential turning point in the market. For them, Australia could be waltzing to the same tune as it did in the 1890s.

### A WATCHING BRIEF

Over the course of 130 years, Australia's housing stock has grown from literally nothing to become among the most expensive in the world. Much of this journey seems to follow the path we have seen in earlier chapters. House prices *can* rise, they *can* beat inflation and they *can* provide a good investment. But for most of the period, house prices rose very slowly, barely beating inflation, and providing a pitiful real return. Between 1880 and 1995 house prices rose at 0.9% per year – a rate similar to that which we have seen elsewhere.

And as elsewhere there has been a recent boom, which looks very different from the previous century or more. But totally unlike recent US history, this boom has continued in Australia. This might be down to economic growth or population shifts, or it might be driven by where people choose to invest, low interest rates or higher levels of debt. Perhaps it is simply speculation. Or, given the extent of the upswing, maybe it is the combined result of all of these things.

It will be fascinating to see whether Australia's record high price levels can continue to rise or whether they will plateau at a new, permanently higher level. Or maybe it is a bubble that will burst. Given the unpredictability of the story so far, trying to guess the ending is perhaps as risky as digging for gold.[12]

For the next stop on our journey we will move from the gold mines of Australia to the Golden Age of seventeenth-century Amsterdam, where we will look at how house prices have changed over the last four centuries.

# CHAPTER 5

# A GOLDEN AGE OF HOUSE PRICES

IF SOMEONE STOPPED YOU IN the street today and asked you to pick anywhere in the world to make a property investment, you might need a moment to think. Would you favour the old guard of cities like New York, Sydney or London? Or would your mind wander to an emerging market like Brazil, India or China? If someone had asked the same question four hundred years ago, though, there would have been no hesitation: your answer would have been Amsterdam.

In 1611 Amsterdam was simmering with activity. The northern Dutch provinces had broken away from Spanish rule and were enjoying the right to live and work in relative freedom. Amsterdam held its arms wide open to newcomers, regardless of their faith or heritage, and quickly gained a reputation for tolerance that survives to this day. Its new inhabitants were a mix of Jewish, Protestant and other Christian movements from all over Europe, including the Pilgrim Fathers, who settled there before sailing for the New World in 1620. Those who stayed in the city brought with them the skills and wealth that would lay the foundation for a Golden Age in Dutch history.

One family making the switch to Amsterdam were the van Alderwerelts, cotton traders originally from nearby Flanders.[1]

When the head of the family, Jan van Alderwerelt, arrived on the outskirts of the city in 1614 he was looking to buy a place to live, and just like any other buyer, he would probably have wanted to study the housing market before making a decision. Unfortunately for him, much of Amsterdam was still a building site and there was precious little housing – let alone a housing market to analyse. Fortunately for us, however, if you walk through Amsterdam today you can see the house he ended up living in, along with most of the other houses built at the same time along the same canal – many of which have barely changed since. As we will see, it makes for an ideal place to investigate house prices.

Jan van Alderwerelt's house, along with nearly five hundred other neighbouring properties, was the subject of a monumental study to celebrate the city of Amsterdam's 750th anniversary in 1975 and published in a weighty book titled *Vier eeuwen Herengracht* ('Four Centuries of the Herengracht').[2] The study uncovered the name of every owner and the prices at which they bought and sold their houses from 1973 all the way back to 1628 – a total of more than 4,000 transactions. For Professor Piet Eichholtz of Maastricht University this presented an opportunity too good to miss. By looking at the changes in prices of these properties over time, he has been able to construct an index of house prices spanning four centuries.[3]

And not only that: because most of the houses are still houses today, with only minor changes to building quality and function, the index can directly compare prices for the same property over a long period. As we have seen, 'repeat-sales' analysis avoids all the adjustments needed in most other indices – we do not need to worry about adjusting for changing size, quality or location. And if we are in any doubt, we can walk down the street and check any particular house for ourselves to see if it has changed much from the house recorded in the historical documents. And we can track the stories of the people that lived in these houses and see how house prices affected their lives.

Professor Eichholtz's study thus provides us with the most accurate historical house price index we are ever likely to find.

It traces Amsterdam's ups and downs through the ages, providing a unique perspective from which to view current-day price movements.

## THE HOUSE THAT JAN BUILT

In the 1620s, the Dutch Republic was well on its way to overtaking Spain and asserting itself as the pre-eminent global power of the seventeenth century. The Dutch had become the middlemen for international trade: ships would embark from there for the Americas, the East Indies (modern-day Indonesia), Japan and Africa, returning with anything from diamonds to saffron or silk.

Nowhere was this economic revolution more evident than in Amsterdam. Its success made the city home to a host of world firsts. In the Dutch East India Company it had the world's first multinational corporation, which held a Dutch monopoly on trade with Asia for two centuries. The company was financed by shares traded on the first modern stock exchange – which itself was supported by the Bank of Amsterdam, a forefather of the modern-day central bank. Amsterdam had grown unrecognizably over the previous half century. Its population had more than trebled from 30,000 to around 100,000. And all the while, people and money continued to flood in.

In response to the roaring demand, Amsterdam was embarking on one of the most ambitious urban planning schemes in history, expanding the city to more than double its original size. City leaders mapped out three concentric canals to surround the city and provide infrastructure for new housing lots – a project that would take nearly a hundred years to complete (see figures 5.1 and 5.2). Throughout, the plan was for the area around the canal closest to the old city to be the most upmarket location in the whole of Amsterdam, away from the dirty business of trade. This was the Herengracht – the gentleman's canal – and the place where Jan van Alderwerelt chose to build his house.

**Figure 5.1.** Urbanization, Dutch-style: Amsterdam in 1609 surrounded by fields.

*Source*: Amsterdam City Archives.

The van Alderwerelts were clearly well off. Buying property in the most desirable location in the world's most desirable city was not cheap. But the fact that the Herengracht has always been a very desirable place to live in Amsterdam provides another advantage of this study. When we compare the price of Jan van Alderwerelt's house with later prices, we can focus on what is happening to the price of the house and not the desirability of the area – imagine if we tried looking at houses in places that have changed markedly over the years, such as Soho in London or Times Square in New York. The main difference between the Herengracht of old and the Herengracht of today is its occupiers: in the seventeenth and eighteenth century they were merchants and shipping brokers from all over the continent, later they were government ministers and railway entrepreneurs, and now they are investment bankers and celebrities. Yet all these inhabitants of the Herengracht have one thing in common: wealth.

**Figure 5.2.** Amsterdam again in 1675, surrounded by three canals, including Herengracht.

*Source*: Amsterdam City Archives.

## ON TOP OF THE WORLD

In 1614 Jan van Alderwerelt bought two plots side by side for 2,260 Dutch guilders and started building a house that would later be replaced by two houses – numbers 60 and 62 on the Herengracht.* But as soon as he finished building, van Alderwerelt began preparing to move out. He had plans for the plot next door, and sold 60/62 to a merchant and started work on what would be number 64 (see figures 5.3 and 5.4).

Perhaps with an eye to the future, and no doubt representing the exuberant confidence of Amsterdam at that time, he built this

---

*The Dutch guilder was introduced in the 1680s and lasted until it was replaced by the euro in 2002. A guilder was worth a set amount of gold or silver until 1936, when the gold standard was abandoned. It is confusingly abbreviated to 'f' or 'fl.', an abbreviation for florin, which was one of the coins it replaced. Values before 1680 are translatable into guilders by converting into gold or silver and then guilders and inflating them with a price index.

72–70          68          66          64          62          60

**Figure 5.3.** The house that Jan built. The distinctive facade of number 64 stands out.

*Source*: Amsterdam City Archives.

**Figure 5.4.** The same houses as in figure 5.3 today.

house with a globe and a cross on the top. The globe above number 64 was so recognizable that the house became known simply as 'De Werelt' or 'the world' – and to some people at the time, such a name would not have seemed overblown: it was the most spectacular house in Europe's most fashionable city. And so, in 1625 Jan van Alderwerelt moved in with his wife and five sons.

He also bought the other neighbour's house, number 68. This house he rented out to a widow, Clara van Bueren, described in *Vier eeuwen Herengracht* as 'the rich widow of the merchant Otto van Bueren'. With his growing buy-to-let portfolio, Jan seems to have been less keen on keeping up with the Joneses and more keen just to buy them out.*

In these early years of the Herengracht the Dutch economy continued to soar and the real, inflation-adjusted prices of houses on the Herengracht doubled between 1628 and 1633. While part of this early gain may have been due to the development profit that normally comes with building a house in a new area, such a rise is rare, as we have seen in previous chapters. Indeed, it would not be repeated for 350 years. Jan van Alderwerelt died in 1633, aged 47. He had seen prices rise throughout his life; it was now time for his children and grandchildren to see what was in store next.

### TULIP MANIA

Jan left his house to his first-born son, also called Jan, who was about to witness another world first in Amsterdam: the first asset bubble. With the highest incomes in Europe, the Dutch had taken to speculating on pretty much anything, particularly tulip bulbs.[4] The flower had been introduced to the country from Turkey a century before and its vibrant, exciting colours and patterns rapidly made it a coveted luxury item, with different varieties providing symbols of social status. They were rare, curious and enormously expensive. The wealthiest citizens were particularly transfixed by the most famous and desirable variety, the *Semper Augustus*, which

---

*Number 68 had a link with number 64 in that it also had a stone facade representing the world, but later the links would become stronger as Jan's son, Pieter, would marry Clara, the daughter of Otto and Clara van Bueren in 1644.

was provided by just one supplier. Moreover, because the bulbs were uprooted and moved around from June to September, during the rest of the year traders had to make up for the excess demand by providing contracts that allowed people to purchase tulips in advance – these were the world's first derivatives, making them ripe for speculation.

It was not only professional traders who gambled on the prices of tulips: so did ordinary citizens. From late in 1636 to early the following year, the speculation reached heights that we struggle to understand today. With the bulbs still in the ground, the price for one pound of bulbs shot up from 20 Dutch guilders to over 1,200 guilders – a change from €350 to €21,000 in today's money – in many cases for bulbs that did not even exist. At a time when the average yearly income was between 200 and 400 guilders, the corrupting power of the flower was clear. The famous *Semper Augustus* variety rose in price from 2,000 guilders for one bulb to 6,000 guilders – as valuable as some of the houses on the Herengracht. One commentator at the time was moved enough to note: 'No one speaks, asks about or talks of anything but flora, so that they have their heads full of it. They can neither think nor dream of anything else.'[5]

On 3 February 1637, the bottom dropped out of the market. People began to realize that many of the bulbs they had bought would never be delivered and the prices of the more common bulbs never recovered. The Dutch called it *Tulpenwoerde*, tulip mania.[6]

The economy was unable to withstand such a collapse. Two years earlier, the plague had begun to sweep through the country, claiming 17,000 lives in 1636 in Amsterdam alone – around one out of every seven people. Real demand for houses was falling, and tulip mania reduced people's desire and ability to speculate. By 1637, real house prices were 40% lower than they had been at their peak in 1633 when Jan Senior had died.

Yet for the van Alderwerelts, who survived the plague, housing turned out to be a safer place for their money than tulips or many other investments. In 1648, the Eighty Years' War with

**Figure 5.5.** Real house prices in Amsterdam before the Napoleonic Wars. *Data source*: Eichholtz.

Spain, that had for a long time been on the periphery of the Nether-lands, came to an end, with the Dutch Republic being recognized abroad for the first time. For the next decade trade flourished, reaching its zenith in the 1650s. While Spain and England were busy going off to war with one another, trade in the Dutch Repub-lic flourished. This is reflected in the Herengracht house price index, which reached its seventeenth-century peak in the 1660s, as can be seen in figure 5.5. In 1663, Jan van Alderwerelt Junior sold 64 Herengracht for 30,000 guilders to his younger brother Pieter. The price had risen by two-thirds since 1640.*

That particular deal is unlikely to have made for a pleas-ant discussion topic at family gatherings, however, as the price almost immediately plummeted. With England's economic and political power beginning to catch up, it increasingly viewed the

---

*Number 64 Herengracht was rented by a successful merchant from Stras-bourg called Frederick Rihel. A monument to the wealth along the Herengracht at that time survives today in the National Gallery in London. At three metres by two metres, Rembrandt's portrait of Frederick Rihel dominates the room it is in. Rihel is shown on horseback wearing cuffs of gold thread.

Netherlands as a rival and put in place a series of Navigation Acts designed to damage Dutch trade. In 1672 England and France almost simultaneously declared war on the Dutch Republic. By early summer, invading troops were less than twenty miles from Amsterdam. A deep financial crisis followed, almost breaking out into civil war. The Herengracht index shows this clearly: from 1670 to 1676 houses prices plummeted by more than half.

But the van Alderwerelts were in no rush to sell. Even with the threat of enemy troops marching through the city, they stayed put and soon received their reward when prices edged back up again. This can be seen with the house of Adriaen van Alderwerelt, who was Jan Junior's son and Jan Senior's grandson. A diamond trader, he had bought another house on the canal, 20 Herengracht, in 1669 for 20,150 guilders. Thirty years later, upon the death of his widow, the house was sold for 28,100 guilders – a rise of just under one-third.* So, again, provided they could survive, housing seemed a safe option for the van Alderwerelts.

The seventeenth century had been a volatile one for house prices in Amsterdam. This was partly because of the ups and downs of trade, which was essential to the city's wealth and which had been disrupted by financial crises, disease and war. Yet by the end of the century, the Netherlands had established itself as a trading hub and a global power. Spanish and French ambitions had been thwarted, and the country's problems with England were temporarily resolved when one of its noblemen, William of Orange, crossed the channel to win the English throne by marrying the King's daughter Mary and staging a bloodless coup d'état in 1688.† But the Golden Age was drawing to a close. Over the next century the Netherlands would find its preeminence under threat from England and France.

---

*Over those thirty years prices rose by about 15%, so a part of the gain was just nominal. 28,500 guilders would be around €450,000 today.

†By 1693 the two monarchs of England founded William and Mary University in Virginia in the American colonies. The second-oldest college in the US, it would go on to educate sixteen signatories to the Declaration of Independence.

## FADING GLORY

The eighteenth century was less volatile for Amsterdam but also less glorious. The price of Jan van Alderwerelt's main house, number 64, mirrors the decline. In 1731, Jacob Daams, the widower of Jan Senior's great granddaughter, sold half the house for 15,200 Dutch guilders – valuing the house at barely any more than the 30,000 guilders that Pieter van Alderwerelt bought it for sixty years earlier.*

The early 1700s had seen euphoric optimism over the new trade opportunities in South America, with several companies set up to take advantage of dwindling Spanish power in the region. Yet when investors started to lose confidence there and elsewhere in Europe, the result was a financial crisis that rippled through the continent – causing a wave of losses in Amsterdam's financial sector. In 1738 house prices along the Herengracht peaked. The part of number 64 that was still owned by the van Alderwerelt family was sold in 1751 for 10,000 guilders, valuing the property at just 20,000 guilders. In twenty years the nominal price had fallen by a third and the real price had fallen even further. But it turned out to be a good time for the van Alderwerelts to sell: prices would reach their 1740s levels once more in 1778 and then not again for 250 years. The middle of the eighteenth century marked the beginning of a period of plodding decline that would continue for the next two centuries.

It was around this time that the Dutch East India Company, which had enjoyed a monopoly on trade in Asia, began to run into financial difficulty. This put strain on the Dutch government, who had bailed it out, further undermining the financial sector. The Dutch difficulties with England also re-emerged at this time,

*Along the canal at number 68 things were changing too. Clara had died in 1704 and had left the house to seven grandchildren: the children of her son Jan Pieter van Alderwerelt. As no doubt happens in many such cases, they had rented the house out for some years, but in 1740 they sold the house by auction and it was bought by 'the immensely rich grain merchant' Barend Luykink. After that time the house moved out of the van Alderwerelt family but has continued being bought, sold and lived-in to the present day.

culminating in the Fourth Anglo-Dutch War between 1780 and 1784, fought over the Dutch support of the American side in their War of Independence. Unlike the Americans, however, the war ended disastrously for the Dutch and effectively ended their status as a great power.

By the time of the Napoleonic Wars at the turn of the nineteenth century house prices were no higher than they had been 150 years earlier. If you look again at figure 5.5, despite all that volatility there is very little ultimate gain to show for it. If you start in 1628, the index does rise by about 0.6% each year up to 1792, but a large part of this rise was due to the growth during the first few years after the houses were built. It is probably fairer to say that house price growth was somewhere between 0.6% each year and nothing.

That rise is hardly impressive. But we should also bear in mind that this average hides periods of gain and loss. Prices over the period moved in a range that was sometimes one-third above that average and sometimes one-third below it. Some, like Jan van Alderwerelt Senior, bought as prices were rising, but others, like the people who bought number 64 in the middle of eighteenth century, could not have picked a worse time to buy.


## NAPOLEON ON THE MARCH

Things were about to get even tougher for the Netherlands. As the war with England ended in 1784, many Dutch citizens, inspired by the Declaration of Independence and the establishment of a constitution in America, started to demand more rights themselves. For a while these aspirations were ruthlessly suppressed. However, next door, the French Revolution caused a seismic shift in Europe and encouraged a popular uprising in the Netherlands that overthrew the old Dutch Republic and set up what would be known as the Batavian Republic. It had been created with the support of the French army that had invaded the Netherlands, and in reality it made the country a puppet state of France, as was

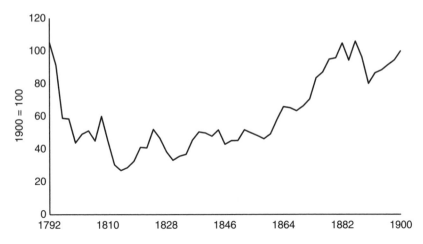

**Figure 5.6.** Real house prices in Amsterdam between the Napoleonic Wars and 1900.

*Data source*: Eichholtz.

clear when Napoleon appointed his brother as King of Holland in 1806. As you might imagine, being a wealthy homeowner in the Herengracht during this time was not as appealing as it had been in the past.

By the time of the Battle of Waterloo in the summer of 1815 houses had lost nearly three-quarters of their value in real terms, compared with their pre-French Revolution prices of 1792, as can be seen in figure 5.6. This huge fall was from the values that, while volatile, had been fairly firmly established over the previous 150 years. In 1802, half of 64 Herengracht was sold for 8,000 guilders. The same half of the property had been sold for more than 15,000 guilders seventy years earlier.

It was only during the second half of the nineteenth century – when Amsterdam started industrializing, people's incomes doubled and population growth recovered – that house prices gradually improved. In 1853, the combined 64 Herengracht sold for 15,800 guilders, just three-quarters of its value a century earlier, but twenty years later the same house would sell for 19,500 guilders.

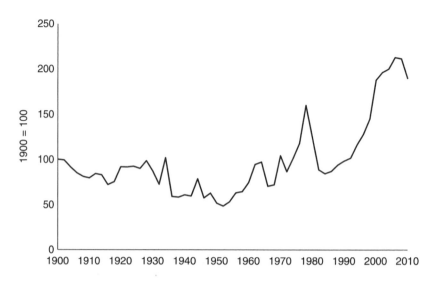

**Figure 5.7.** Real house prices in Amsterdam since 1900.
*Data sources*: Eichholtz; NMV; Central Bureau for Statistics.

By the end of the nineteenth century, however, house prices had only recovered to the levels of a hundred years earlier. Someone who had bought a house in 1814 would have seen an annual real increase of 1.5% up to 1900, and would no doubt have been very pleased with their investment in property. But with our longer perspective we can also see that house prices in 1900 were only at the same real level that they had been in 1646 – more than 250 years earlier.

### INTO LIVING MEMORY

House price movements in Amsterdam over the twentieth century (see figure 5.7) exhibit many of the patterns we have seen elsewhere, with prices declining unevenly until after the Second World War. Despite the Netherlands remaining neutral in the First World War, it suffered from wartime shortages as well as postwar inflation, influenza and an economic slump. It was affected, like other cities across the world, by the Great Depression and the effects of this lingered up until the Second World War. In 1940 Hitler's forces did not respect Dutch neutrality, and unlike 1914, the Netherlands suffered invasion and occupation. Houses lost a hefty 40% of their real value between 1900 and the 1940s, but perhaps this was understandable given the ordeals that the country had suffered.

The general story of rising house prices in the forty years up to 1900 and then their fall for the next forty years was reflected at another of Jan van Alderwerelt's former houses: 60 Herengracht. In 1850, the businessman Hendrik Salm purchased the house for 20,600 guilders. When he died in 1863 his widow sold the house to commissioner August von der Heide for 31,200 guilders as the economy began to recover. In 1881, Eduard Kluinders, the director of a railway company, purchased the house for 46,500 guilders. But from the turn of the century, prices started to fall. The house first passed to a furniture trader, W. Petersmann, for 37,000 guilders, and then, in 1911, to an exporter of luxury goods called Hermann Garschagen for 36,000 guilders. Although the house was bought by a mortgage bank for 45,000 guilders in 1935, it was sold on in 1939 for 40,000 guilders. In ninety years the nominal price had doubled but the real price had only risen by a quarter – a yearly rate of only around 0.3%.

House prices gradually improved after the Second World War, with a rise to accompany the resources boom in the 1970s as the Netherlands discovered large natural gas reserves. It was a borrowers' market as mortgage lending criteria were relaxed, interest rates were held low to prevent exchange rates from rising and optimism prevailed. Yet as the 1979 international recession started to bite, and as the regulators reversed these more relaxed lending criteria, the market slumped again. The correction was swift and sizeable, with nominal house prices falling by 30% and real prices halving.

By 1992 prices had rebounded and were back to their 1974 level – which was also the 1900 level. If you had bought a house along the Herengracht in 1952, the real price of your property would have risen by an average of 1.9% per year up to 1992. While this is not a bad return, beneath that average were periods of great volatility. Even more striking is the fact that the identical real price levels of 1992 and 1970 were not only the same as that of 1900 – they were also identical to the price level of 1646. Across four hundred years real house price levels had been flat.

Looking at the period since the early 1990s, we also see the same story as elsewhere, with a very substantial increase in house prices. Between 1990 and the peak in 2007, prices tripled in nominal terms and doubled in real terms. But since the 2007 peak, prices have fallen back by nearly 15%, though they are still at record highs. Thanks to Professor Eichholtz's study, we can see that this goes against the course of house prices over four hundred years. As he points out, focusing on the last fifty years poses a problem: it is only one part of a much longer history.

### A BETTER WORD FOR 'BUBBLE'

Between 1628 (when the index begins) and 2010 (the latest available data at the time of writing), nominal house prices in Amsterdam have risen nearly twentyfold, with most of the nominal rise being caused by the inflation after the Second World War. Yet what is more striking about this index is what it tells us about *real* prices. In figure 5.8 we can see prices evolve over four centuries. Even if we measure from the below-trend level of 1628 to the above-trend level of 2010, the real annual increase is a measly 0.4%. A more realistic interpretation of the index is that prices are probably a bit better than flat, albeit with some fairly large swings. But this flatness over such a long period goes against our pre-held beliefs about how house prices behave.

Rather than painting a picture of increasing prices, the graphs reveal a great deal of volatility. Speaking to *The New York Times*, Professor Eichholtz suggested that using the metaphor of a bubble to describe what is happening now in housing markets is wrong. 'What you see is rising and falling, sometimes dramatically,

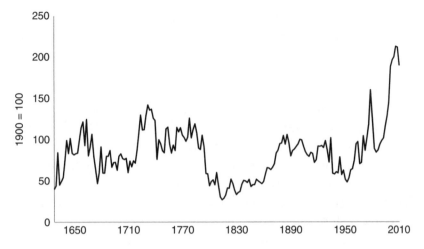

**Figure 5.8.** Real house prices in Amsterdam over four centuries.
*Data sources*: Eichholtz; NMV; Central Bureau for Statistics.

depending on whether the city had a stable economy or became hostage to outside forces. That's not a bubble bursting – it's volatility.'[7]

Unsurprisingly, there is much debate in the Netherlands at the moment as to where house prices will go next. Some experts argue that the current market prices are supported by fundamentals: the rate of economic growth, shortage of supply, low interest rates and so on.[8] Others argue that the market is massively overvalued – some claim that it is overvalued by up to 100%.* Judging who is right will be another task for historians in the years to come.

Eichholtz's study is compelling, not just because of the care with which it has been compiled but also because we can go and see the very same houses to which it refers. On a walk around the Herengracht today you will pass the same houses that we have reviewed here. The house which Jan van Alderwerelt sold

---

*For example, William Xu-Doeve argues that households will be unable to afford to finance the costs of house purchases at the present level and that this will become worse as interest rates are likely to rise. As financing costs increase, he argues, the maximum price people will be able to pay for a house will fall.[9]

to his brother in 1663 for 30,000 guilders still stands. Adjusted for inflation, their transaction is worth about half a million euros in today's money.* The prices along the Herengracht today are nearer €2 million – at this price, houses have increased at an annual real rate of 0.4%.

But we will have to wait for a few years to see if the index remains at its current highs or if it falls back towards its historical levels. If Dutch house prices were to revert to this long-term trend, they would have to fall by a very large amount. Given the already-high levels of mortgage debt in the country, such a fall would have severe consequences for homeowners, their families and the banking system that has lent to them. But if prices do not fall back in the longer term, we will have a period that will be at odds with four hundred years of history.

And our journey continues even further back in time as we take a short train-ride to France, one of the countries that had such an influence on Dutch house prices at key points, and which we will see has had equally turbulent periods in its history and its housing market.

*Or, given that 30,000 guilders bought 18,000 grammes of gold at that time, valuing it using today's gold price gives a figure of €600,000.

# CHAPTER 6

# PARISIAN HOUSE PRICES: EIGHT-HUNDRED YEARS OF DÉJÀ VU

SO FAR IN THIS BOOK we have travelled through a century of house prices in the US, Norway and Australia and through four centuries in Amsterdam. For our longest look back in time, our journey takes us to France, and in particular to Paris, a city that has been a major centre for trade and civilization for many hundreds of years. We will look over eight hundred years of wars, famines and revolutions that have seen empires come and go, kings and queens lose their heads, invading armies march through the streets and, despite all that, the maintenance of a proud culture and the emergence of modern-day France. Bringing together this treasure trove of data was a truly historic task and we have three generations of French economists working a century apart to thank for doing so.

The foundations were laid by Georges d'Avenel (1855–1939), who, at the end of the nineteenth century, began investigating transaction prices in Paris from 1200 to 1800, averaging them to produce estimates of property prices in twenty-five-year intervals.[1] Building on this was Gaston Duon (1908–2005), a researcher at the French statistical office during the Second World War. A pioneer of the 'repeat sales' method, Duon gained access to property registers kept by the tax department and was able to construct an index for the centre of Paris in ten-year increments from 1790 to 1850.[2] By connecting his data to his predecessor's, he was able to go back to 1625 (the same year the Amsterdam Herengracht index started). And with richer data for more recent years, he was able to calculate a year-by-year index from 1840 to 1944.

Duon also developed our understanding of house prices by estimating how much their values change as a result of getting old or being in need of repair. In 1943, Duon compared the prices of buildings that were located in the same districts but built in different periods. He saw that the older buildings were losing around 20% of their value every twenty years for reasons as mundane as the roof needing to be patched up, window frames needing to be painted or bricks needing to be repointed. He therefore created an adjusted index for what he called the 'obsolescence' of housing stock and this differs by 0.7% each year from his unadjusted index. His work makes the important point that owning a house is not free of costs: we all know that there are a series of bills that we need to pay to keep our homes in shape, and these costs eat into any gains we make.

The third generation of economists to explore house prices in France is led by Jacques Friggit, who brings us up to the present day. A senior French civil servant and economist, he has connected the previous indices to those which are now calculated on a rolling basis by the French statistics office. Taking their work together, then, we have an index of Parisian property prices that covers every year since 1840, every ten-year period since 1790 and every twenty-five-year period since the thirteenth century. The combined effort required to create this index took over a hundred years – and the work continues.

It will come as no surprise, however, to find that the large time span covered has left room for error – particularly in the early centuries. For this reason, most economists consider the later parts of the index to be the most accurate. Nevertheless, the broad sweep of house prices over such a long period can help us in our examination of how house prices behave over the long term – and you will not get much longer term than this.

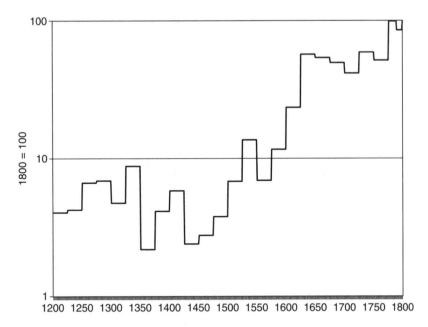

**Figure 6.1.** Paris real house prices from 1200 to 1800 in twenty-five-year intervals.

*Data source*: d'Avenel (CGEDD).[1]

## HOUSE PRICES IN PARIS, 1200–1800

D'Avenel's index starts in 1200 and looks only at central Paris (see figure 6.1). Furthermore, while he did perform some adjustments for quality differences, these must have been at best approximations. The broad picture, however, is that houses in 1800 were twenty-two times more expensive than they had been six hundred years earlier. While the headline seems impressive, this represents an annual real increase of only 0.5% over the period – and over the first three hundred of these years, prices actually fell in real terms.

Between 1350 and 1450, the French king was embroiled in the Hundred Years' War with England. France also suffered the devastation of the Black Death. Naturally, house prices did not do too well either.

By the sixteenth century, religious wars notwithstanding, France began a period of relative peace. By annexing formerly independent regions such as Brittany, establishing French as the common language and setting up colonies in the New World, France was starting to take its place on the world stage. France's growing economic and political success during this century is reflected in the rise in Parisian property prices, with prices continuing to grow through the mid 1600s.

But the peace did not last. With Louis XIV now in power, war with the Dutch Republic broke out in 1672 and lasted until 1678. The war was extremely costly for both sides, and just as we saw earlier with house prices in Amsterdam, Parisian house prices fell. Following all this, France was hit by two crippling famines between 1693 and 1710 that killed over two million people.[3] House prices that had been rising for the previous two centuries now ground to a halt.

## REVOLUTIONARY IDEAS

As the eighteenth century unfolded, France prospered and so did house prices. But as the century reached its final quarter, the fortunes of those living in France depended on their varying circumstances. Trade in Paris was flourishing, supporting the growth of a bourgeois class of merchants – but one whose wealth was not reflected in their political power. The lives of peasants, meanwhile, had barely improved and they had just suffered the crop failures of 1788. The government, having come to the aid of the Americans in their campaign for independence, had stretched its finances to near crisis point. As the social strife reached a tipping point, it set in motion a defining period in world history: the French Revolution.

From 1789, France underwent a decade of radical social and political change. Class conflict spilt out into violence on the streets, and the instability led to war with several of France's neighbours. In 1792, the French monarchy was abolished, the First Republic proclaimed and, a year later, both Louis XVI and his wife, Marie Antoinette, were guillotined. House prices did not suffer the same fate, instead remaining flat throughout the turmoil.

### ENTER NAPOLEON

Fighting during these wars that followed the Revolution was a young general, Napoleon Bonaparte, who would soon seize power and establish himself as Emperor of France, ushering in a period of French domination in Europe.

One of the many changes that occurred in Europe was that the Netherlands became a French territory, causing the houses along the Herengracht canal in Amsterdam to fall compared with those in Paris. Yet Paris's rise was still closely allied with the fortunes of the country as a whole. The Napoleonic Wars ended in defeat and the eventual exile of Napoleon in 1815. After a slight increase in house prices, the uncertainty helped sour the market and prices fell.

But France's power was not crushed, and nor were the Bonapartes. Following an unsuccessful return to monarchy, Napoleon's nephew returned from his exile in Switzerland and rose to power in 1850. Napoleon III's reign oversaw a return to prosperity and house prices rose sharply again, but – as with his uncle – military defeat was ruinous. In 1871, the victors of the Franco-Prussian War ordered a war indemnity of around 20% of French output, forcing the French government to borrow heavily. This increased the interest rates payable on government bonds and investors switched out of housing to benefit from these more attractive rates. The result was a sudden fall in demand for property and, consequently, in property prices.

Looking at Duon's index in figure 6.2, we see that another rise was soon to follow. The industrial revolution was spreading across Europe and a physical manifestation of this movement – the railway – was a major force in modernizing rural France

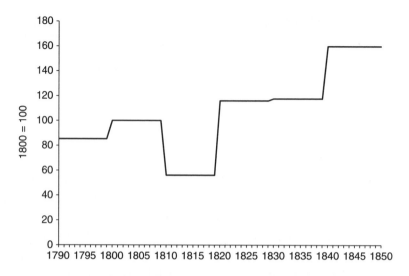

**Figure 6.2.** Paris real house prices, 1790–1850.
*Data source*: Duon (CGEDD).[2]

and boosting the country's economic prospects. This hastened urbanization and Paris grew as a result, with large parts of the city remodelled and the creation of its trademark boulevards. In 1889, the International Exhibition to commemorate one hundred years since the Revolution was held in Paris. At its gateway stood the magnificent and unique Eiffel Tower, then the largest man-made structure in the world. It must have felt like a new dawn for France.

Over the period from 1840 to 1900 real house prices in Paris rose an average of 1.7% each year, with prices roughly doubling in the last quarter of the century (see figure 6.3). In the previous six hundred years, prices had increased at a much slower rate – around 0.5% in real terms per year – and at that rate it took two hundred years for prices to increase by the same proportion they did in the sixty years to 1900. For property owners this must have felt like a golden age. Let us hope they enjoyed it while it lasted. By the start of the Second World War all of those gains would be lost, with prices tumbling back down to their 1840 levels.

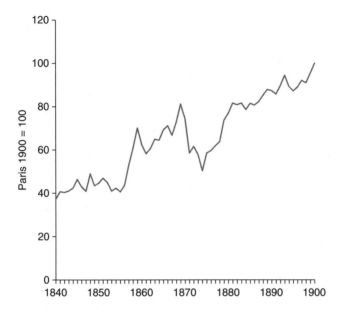

**Figure 6.3.**  Real house prices in Paris, 1840–1900.
*Data source*: Friggit (CGEDD).[4]

### THE LONGEST FALL

At the onset of the First World War, the political emphasis was on keeping the war brief and victorious – to restore national pride following defeat forty years earlier. As part of this war plan, landlords were willing to accept government legislation that effectively froze rents in the city, thus making houses a less attractive investment for owners of capital. Even worse, inflation during the war saw the price of goods rise three times over, such that by the end of the war rents were one-third of their prewar level in real terms. As a result, buildings lost two-thirds of their *real* value. Even after the war, the government, through fear of unpopularity, did not lift the rent controls. With further rapid inflation, real house prices continued their steep decline.

France was then devastated by the Great Depression. In the first two years of the 1930s, output in France fell by nearly a third and took most of the decade to recover. And yet the Paris index actually increased significantly, mirroring what we have seen in other countries during the early 1930s. Analysis from that time suggests that this can partly be explained by a relaxation of rent controls in the late 1920s, but mostly it can be put down to the flight of investors to the supposed safety of housing investment after the 1929 stock market crash reminded them of stock volatility.[5] It seems that the idea of houses being 'as safe as houses' was held by many a French investor. Yet again, though, this price rise was short lived. In 1935 the government imposed a compulsory 10% rent cut as part of an openly deflationary policy and by 1938 the rise in house prices had vanished.

During the Second World War the government implemented rent controls, as it had during the First. The occupation of Paris added a second blow to prices, with a third coming from the inflation that accompanied the rationing of goods. As the allied armies fought their way across France in 1944 and 1945, freeing France from occupation, the economy, as well as much of the country's infrastructure, was wrecked. Savings were sparse, credit hard to obtain and regulations on rents continued to choke the market. Against this background, house prices continued to fall until the late 1940s.

Unsurprisingly, the low rents from 1914 until after the Second World War meant that homeowners and landlords were reluctant to invest in the upkeep of their properties. A number of commentators discuss the very poor standard of French properties after the war. If Duon's obsolescence rule of thumb is correct, house prices might have fallen by 20–30% because of the widespread disrepair.

The period from the start of the First World War to about 1950 saw the most prolonged and severe fall in house prices that we have seen in our review of any country at any time (see figure 6.4). The *real* price of a house in 1950 was only one-fifth of what it had been in 1939, and one-tenth of the pre-1914 price level. Prices were at about the same level as they had been in the seventeenth century, three hundred years before. France had suffered one blow after another: the First World War, rent controls, inflation, the

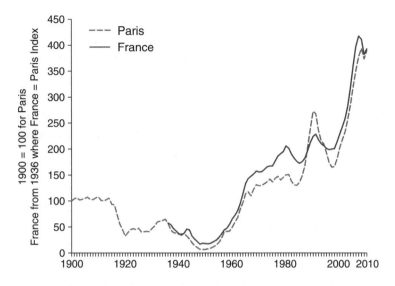

**Figure 6.4.** Real house prices in France, 1900–2010.
*Data source*: Friggit (CGEDD).

Great Depression, the Second World War, German occupation, economic desolation and crumbling housing stock. No wonder house prices collapsed. This was certainly an unfortunate series of events and we would all hope that the chances of a repeat are slim, but it does show us how far and for how long house prices are able to fall.

### A TURNING POINT

By 1948 the rent controls had been kept so low that the average worker was said 'to spend more money to pay for his cigarettes than for his rent'.[6] As laws began to give landlords more freedom to set rents, house prices managed to escape from their lull. The result was that the house price index recovered briskly between 1950 and 1965. Not for the first time in this book, we have seen how the combination of war and government intervention placed a stranglehold on the market.

At this point, our index begins to collate data from the French statistical office. The fast postwar growth ended in 1965, forming what our third economist, Jacques Friggit, calls a 'turning point' in the house price index. For the following thirty-five years, the ratio of house prices relative to disposable income per household remained flat, moving only 10% up or down and always returning to trend. A short-term deviation took place in Paris and a few other cities in the late 1980s and early 1990s when house prices spiked, mirroring the booms and busts seen in many other developed economies at that time.

Since 2000, however, house prices have been increasing rapidly across all of France. As if to taunt the rule of not moving by more than 10%, by 2010 the house price index relative to average disposable income per household reached 70% higher than the long-term average. A house that would have required a fifteen-year mortgage in 1965 or 2000 would now need a twenty-five-year mortgage. Meanwhile, household mortgage debt has doubled, from 30% of income in the late 1990s to 58% in 2010. At the peak in 2008, the price of an average house was roughly twice what it had been in 2000. And throughout this period, the quality of houses has barely changed.[7]

According to Friggit, changes in supply and demand can explain only part of the rise – with mortgages and low interest rates accounting for barely half the jump. Since 2008, the question marks over house prices in Paris, and in France overall, are the same as those that linger in other developed markets. The same global financial crisis has affected France, with output falling 2.2% in 2009, while the unemployment rate has increased from 7.4% in 2008 to nearly 10% now. House prices, meanwhile, have fallen by around 5–10% since 2008.

## ALL IN THE TIMING

This very long series of house prices in France challenges our belief that houses are a safe and attractive investment. We obviously need to be a little cautious in how we interpret the six hundred years of data from 1200 to 1800, but it is intriguing that this shows a real increase of just 0.5% per year in house prices. For 1840–2000, house prices rise 1% a year – not bad, but not that good either. These levels of increase are similar to the picture we have seen over the long term in the US, Norway, Australia and Amsterdam, but very different from our experience in the UK over our lifetimes.

The idea of steady growth and rules such as 'buy on the dips' could have caused much heartache over the centuries in France, particularly during the 1914–50 period, when buying after a price fall would have been likely to have left you exposed to further falls.

Just as we have done for the UK in the first chapter, Friggit asks whether houses have been a good investment compared with an investment in the stock market.[8] Friggit calculates that if you had invested in the French stock market from 1840 to the present day, you would have received a return of 6.6% each year plus inflation, compared with a trend rate of increase in Parisian housing prices since 1840 of only 1.3% per year. Yet as we have seen in earlier chapters, houses can earn rent or be lived in. Indeed, before the First World War, only 3% of Parisian houses were lived in by their owners. So we should add rental income, averaging 3.3% of the property's value per year, to the returns. This gives a trend figure of around 4.6% plus inflation. However, this is still two percentage points lower than the return on stocks.

As in the UK, it may be that the ability to magnify returns by taking out a mortgage makes housing more attractive for many. The French market clearly shows, however, that prices can easily fall, with dire consequences for investors who have overstretched themselves. Over shorter periods, the housing market has on occasions outperformed stocks – but this requires careful timing, and is particularly difficult to get right when buying and selling houses is such a time-consuming and expensive business.

Friggit also argues that changes in house prices have a high 'autocorrelation'. What this suggests is that a one-off small shock up or down might continue for two or three years but then the effect will die out by year four or year five. A large, ongoing change in the market, like a baby boom, might take longer to unwind, but, crucially, if the factor explaining the rise in prices is not permanent, neither is the rise.

Following this argument, even if the last ten years have shown a rapid increase, house prices should eventually return to their long-term trend. There are other indicators that Friggit argues are signs that the current level of house prices is unsustainable. In particular, he notes the very high current levels of the ratios of house prices to income and to rents. Another indicator is the fact that the French index has generally lagged the US index by one or two years, and, ominously for French house prices, the US index is falling. The two likely scenarios that Friggit outlines are a fast reversal – with nominal prices falling by around 35% in the next five to eight years – or, alternatively, nominal prices remaining the same for the next fifteen to twenty years, with *real* prices being eroded by rising prices. He suspects that the fast reversal is more likely.

Whether history is a good guide to the future is something we will have to wait to find out. So far house prices in France are only slightly down from their peak. We have seen over the last eight hundred years that there are no guarantees that house prices will continue on any particular trend, be it up or down. While we can say with certainty that the current boom differs markedly from the long-term trends, we can also see that house prices are able to move significantly around that long-term trend, sometimes for a generation or more.

If that is not enough to make French homeowners uncertain, they do not need to look very far to find a country in which house prices have taken a completely different path over the last twenty years. That country, Germany, shares with France both a border and an intertwined history, and it is our next stop.

# CHAPTER 7

# GERMAN HOUSE PRICES: A FLAT STORY

## AN ALTERNATIVE VIEW OF THE WORLD

WE HAVE SEEN ELSEWHERE THAT house prices can remain flat in real terms for many decades, if not centuries. But in all the countries we have explored so far, house prices have risen in the last decade or two, even if subsequently many of them have begun to fall. Germany is different. It was flat before the recent boom, and it has been flat throughout it as well. For those that believe the recent house price boom is due to global causes – for example, global economic growth, the emerging-markets boom, lower real interest rates, financial deregulation – Germany stands as an exception to the rule.

And yet over this period it is not as if the German economy has stagnated – quite the reverse. Germany has grown rapidly and is today one of the most prosperous countries in the world. It is an attractive place to live, with several of Germany's cities consistently ranking among the world's most desirable. And it is not as if the German population do not know how to handle their finances – they are careful to build their pensions and their savings. Yet all these positive trends seem to have had little impact on house prices. Germany presents us with a different 'Weltanschauung': a different 'view of the world'.

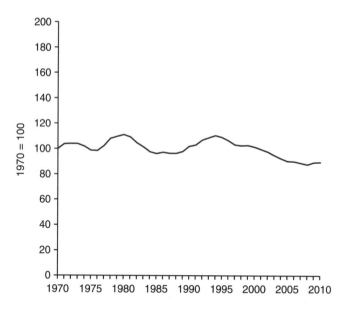

**Figure 7.1.** Real house prices in Germany, 1970–2010.
*Data source*: OECD.[1]

We might expect Germany to be one country where there would be a considerable amount of historical data and analysis about house prices, and it comes as a surprise that the most widely used price indices only go back to about 1989.[2] Fortunately, with the help of the OECD and the German government we have data that goes back to 1970. When you see the data, which is in figure 7.1, the lack of interest in house price changes becomes more understandable: there are virtually no movements. The real prices just move gently along, year after year. With such a history of house prices, anyone investing a great deal of their time in following this index would certainly need to find other interests to keep them stimulated. There are a few gentle rises and a few gentle falls, but even the largest of these represents a move of less than 10% away from trend. What a contrast this is with the turbulent changes Germany has been through over this period.

## BEFORE THE FALL OF THE WALL

Twenty years ago the door to freedom opened up and a seemingly invincible wall that divided a people and an entire continent suddenly became permeable. It was one of the happiest
moments of my life.

Angela Merkel, German Chancellor (November 2009)

All of us who, in 1989, saw the images of the peoples of the two
Germanies pulling down the wall with their hands will not easily
forget that defining moment in Germany's history. No wonder
those directly involved were deeply affected.

The physical divide between the two parts of Germany may
have been just a few slabs of concrete, but economically the dis-
parity was vast. The house price data up to 1990 is for the more
successful West Germany, and even there, despite economic success, house prices were subdued.

After the Second World War, West Germany's economy recovered quickly, aided by the Marshall Plan, a focus on reconstruction
and the influx of foreign workers. It was described as an economic
miracle, and by 1970 West Germany was again one of the leading
economies in the world. The oil price rises of the early 1970s hit
West Germany hard, and unemployment rose. We can see that
real house prices dipped a little. Helmut Schmidt, who became
chancellor in 1974, developed the welfare state further, and house
prices slowly declined. The economic success of West Germany
before reunification brought the country great prosperity but did
little for real house prices, and it was against this backdrop that the
new unified government moved its focus from economic growth
to political reunification.

## AFTER THE FALL OF THE WALL

After the celebrations came the reality. Two economic systems that
had been driving in wildly different directions for nearly half a

century had to be steered as one. Eastern Germany's economy was in a disastrous condition. Factories were dilapidated and machinery had been left to rust. According to once top-secret papers from the planning ministries, less than a fifth of its industry could compete once its economy merged with that of West Germany.[3] The money needed from private investors to rejuvenate the economy was simply not available.

The path of real house prices since reunification shows a slight rise of around 8% from 1990 to the peak in 1994, followed by a steady decline to today, with house prices standing 19% below that peak, or around 10% below the longer-term trend. We can hardly call any of these movements a boom or a crash, but we can try and understand their causes.

Between the fall of the wall in November 1989 and reunification in October the following year, around 600,000 residents of the former German Democratic Republic chose to move west in search of jobs and a brighter future. And the flows continued after reunification, with nearly 10% of the population of former East Germany eventually making the switch.[4] Movements of people at this rate are simply not sustainable and in a bid to hold back the tide, politicians from all sides promised to help the east catch up.

This movement of people put a strain on housing supply in the west, but there was also a shortage of adequate housing in the east. The communist East German government had launched a construction programme in the early 1970s to overcome the shortage that had existed since the 1950s. Overall, three million flats were built, many of these the infamous 'plattenbau': prefabricated slab construction apartment blocks.

Yet by 1989 more than 750,000 surplus requests for new flats revealed that many were still left wanting – especially given the quality of the existing housing stock. In response, public investment flooded in, with the government doubling its spending on housing within five years.[5] Among the government's policies was the 'Development Areas Act', offering generous tax deductions to attract private investment for the construction of new housing and the refurbishment of the crumbling stock. By the mid 1990s the effects could be seen: up went new buildings and up went their prices.

By 1995 the price index for detached homes in former East Germany reached a level of nearly 20% above the 1990 level. But the number of households did not keep up. The average vacancy rate of housing in East Germany more than doubled from 6.2% to roughly 13.2% of total housing, and by 2000 around one million flats were vacant.[6] Between 1996 and 2001, with the number of unsold houses soaring the construction sector slowly wilted. Whereas in 1997 construction firms had built around 180,000 new houses, by 2001 construction was running at a quarter of that level. The government had been caught by surprise. Undersupply had swiftly become oversupply and house prices fell back. Many investors lost their money – something they would not forget.

In 2000 a special commission was set up to develop strategies to handle the oversupply and recommended a policy to lift German prices. It is hard to imagine any politician elsewhere even considering the policy they proposed. They recommended a programme to demolish 350,000 flats and a change in housing policy to cut back the investment incentives. In 2001 a special programme for the East German housing market was introduced offering €60 for the destruction of every square metre of housing space. At the same time, the huge tax credits and grants available for housing construction began to be phased out, having cost the federal government an estimated €35 billion between 1990 and 2008.[7]

While other countries' housing markets have boomed since the mid 1990s, house prices in Germany have actually fallen in real terms. Most of this fall is driven by the east, where house prices have dropped by around 20% since the post-reunification period.

To a large extent, the differences between the east and the west continue. People's spending in the east is on average still 20% behind the spending of those in the west, while unemployment is roughly double.[8] Property prices show the same divide. In 2009, a single family house in Berlin, Germany's capital and largest city with a population of 3.5 million, cost roughly three-quarters of the price of a house in Hamburg, Germany's second-largest city, situated in former West Germany. Way out ahead is the south-western city of Munich, Germany's third largest city but by far its most expensive. Munich may have only four people to every ten Berliners but four of its houses cost the same as ten in Berlin.

## A DIFFERENCE IN ATTITUDE

In Germany, house prices are just not the national obsession that they are in other countries such as the UK. People just do not seem to care as much. Germany's rate of home ownership is 43% – the lowest in the EU and among the lowest in the developed world – and in Berlin the rate is only 15%. In a country where house prices move so little, it is little wonder that there are fewer people interested in them and fewer companies interested in collecting data about them. It is unclear whether the flat real prices cause the lack of interest or if the lack of interest causes the flat real prices. Either way, it seems to be a mutually reinforcing cycle.

This does not mean that Germany has *no* housing market, far from it. There has been a great deal of construction and there are a wide variety of styles of houses and apartments to buy. There is also a very active rental market, with good regulation and security of tenure. Tenants' associations are active in ensuring rental properties are well maintained at a fair cost to tenants. Compared with many other countries this makes renting relatively more attractive.

Germans seem to view housing in a much more functional way. Houses are places to live, not ways of making a fortune. We have seen elsewhere that for property bubbles to occur you first need people to want to speculate on house values, and you also need people to have the funds available to do so. It seems as if that desire to speculate is far less in Germany. And given the history of house prices there, why would anyone rationally think that there were fortunes to be made in waiting for houses to increase in value?

Moreover, for those who do want to buy, finding the money is more difficult than it is in some other countries. Banks in Germany have been more cautious investors in the housing market than banks elsewhere. Mortgages in Germany require a typical down payment of 30–35% of the value of the property, whereas during the boom years in the UK you could take out a mortgage with a deposit of 10% or less. This tighter credit environment means that it would be harder to speculate even if you wanted to – and more importantly, very few do.

Because many in Germany do not expect a capital gain on their house, and because of the high transaction costs, when they buy, Germans tend to be making a long-term decision.* Once someone moves from renting into owning property, that home tends to be the one where they live for the rest of their lives.[9]

### WILL GERMANY CHANGE?

Germany's aging population may be about to change the country's attitude to house prices. With low home ownership, many Germans arrive at retirement still renting. As their income falls, the requirement to still pay rent makes them more likely to be dependent on the state for support. In a country where the population is getting older, this is a serious concern for government finances.

Since 2002, a new state-sponsored pension scheme has been used to promote home ownership among older people. Between €10,000 and €50,000 from a person's accumulated state pension can be used to build or purchase a house in Germany. We will have to wait and see if this incentive raises home ownership among the older members of the population. Even if it does, it is hard to imagine this creating a boom, especially since the forecasts also suggest that the population may decline in the longer term.

---

*Transaction costs in Germany are about 8% of the property's value and are mostly paid by the buyer. In the UK costs are 4%, in the US around 5%, and in France they are often well above 10% (source: OECD).

## A DIFFERENT SET OF BELIEFS

The picture that emerges from Germany is quite different to the one this book started with in the UK. Experience in Germany has shown that house prices do not rise in real terms – if anything, they tend to fall. Prices in Germany have not been particularly volatile so it does not matter much when you buy – that decision is therefore driven by your circumstances, in particular whether you are ready to settle. The economic advantages of getting onto the property ladder are far less convincing.

One important reason for this different set of beliefs is that in Germany inflation does not trick you into believing that you are getting great returns. While Germany had high inflation during the 1970s and around the time of reunification, over the last forty years house prices, even in nominal terms, have risen by only 150%. Over the same period in the UK, nominal house prices have risen by around 4,300%. And for the last fifteen years, German nominal prices have been flat. We saw that real prices were extremely unexciting, and this modest nominal increase, as shown in figure 7.2, might raise the pulse, but not by much.

The German experience raises fundamental questions about why house prices there have behaved so differently than they have elsewhere. What would have needed to happen for Germany to have looked like the UK? Could the UK or the US have chosen to be more like Germany?

German house prices have not seen the increases that we have seen elsewhere. But is this such a bad thing? Instead of investing money in housing, Germans tend to save and invest in industry. Germany was certainly not immune to the credit crunch – a number of its banks had foolishly bought into the US mortgage-backed securities market, it was briefly hit by the global recession, and it is the main funder of the bailouts for Ireland and other countries – but it does not have the problems of an overvalued domestic property market, or any of the issues this causes for banks and credit markets.

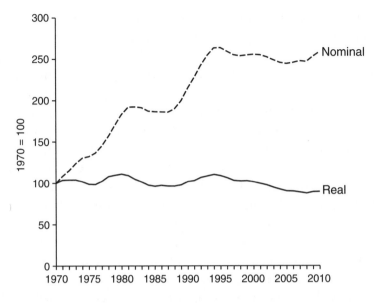

**Figure 7.2.** Nominal and real German house prices, 1970–2010.
*Data source*: OECD.

Germany shows us that the picture of flat real prices that we have seen in other countries in previous decades and centuries is also present today. Germany is not the only example: a similar picture can be seen in Switzerland, Finland, Japan and even Italy. Booms require an upsurge in demand and financing for that demand. And in Germany, given their experience and their beliefs, that upsurge in demand just has not happened. In the next chapter we will examine a number of countries where many were desperate to get into the market and were able to find banks willing to finance them to do so.

## A DIFFERENT DYNAMIC

It may be too simplistic to identify straightforward cause-and-effect reasons why Germany does not have the same house price history that we see in the UK. It may be that it is a combination of factors that together create a very different dynamic. The desire to speculate on houses is much lower than in other countries: partly through experience, partly for cultural reasons, and partly through the absence of inflation's deluding prism. Financing is more conservative, with relatively higher deposits also making speculation more difficult. Supply has tended to meet demand, because building houses for people has been seen as important by successive governments, leading to significant construction programmes where necessary. When combined, these factors have created an environment in which houses are affordable, where renting is the choice of many who are not yet ready to own, and where houses are not seen as a way of generating wealth.

House prices in Germany may present an uneventful story, but housing there is a stable, functional and affordable asset. It lacks the excitement of the boom–bust markets that we have seen elsewhere, but no doubt many potential purchasers will prefer this story. As we will see in the next chapter, too much excitement can be bad for your wealth.

# CHAPTER 8

# RECENT COLLAPSES:
# JAPAN, IRELAND AND SPAIN

## TURNING JAPANESE

IN LATE 2008, WITH THE global financial system perilously close
to collapse, governments received two main warnings from
economists. The first was that countries should act fast to avoid a
rerun of the 1930s. The second was that countries should act fast
to avoid becoming Japan.

That second bit of advice might strike you as odd. Barely
twenty years earlier Japan was being hailed from all corners as
an economic miracle. Despite being a small island with barely
enough natural resources to feed itself, from 1955 to 1970 Japan's
income had grown by a staggering 10% each year.[1] And while
the economy took a hit during the energy crises of the 1970s, by
1980 it had gone from being in the world's second tier to being the
world's second largest economy. At the same time, Tokyo began to
emerge as a major financial centre to rival London and New York
and it started taking advantage of the global trend in financial
deregulation. Far from being used as a warning, Japan's strategy of economic development was held up as an example to be
followed.

But Japan's economic growth flatlined during the 1990s, unemployment soared and the years of wasted opportunities for a generation of Japanese people earned the name the 'lost decade'. And economic performance since the start of the new millennium has only added to the insult: Japan is now living through its 'lost decades'. Alongside its change in fortune has been a boom and bust in the housing market that has dragged the economy, and many ordinary people, down with it.

### PAYING GRANDAD'S DEBTS

Japan's postwar combination of being a fast-growing economy and becoming a fledgling financial centre had taken lending to another level. From 1983 to 1986 house prices had risen by nearly 20%. By the end of the 1980s, lending to companies and households was growing at double-digit annual growth rates.[2] With so much money available, and with asset prices already rising, speculation was inevitable. Japan's stock price index – the Nikkei 225 – began accelerating in 1986, eventually trebling to a peak of ¥38,915 in late 1989. Between 1985 and 1990 real house prices rose by over 35%. At the height of the boom, the grounds of the Imperial Palace in Tokyo, the main residence of the Emperor of Japan, were reportedly worth more than all the real estate in California combined. The grounds are less than ten square kilometres.

In order to help people afford such inflated property prices, lenders in Japan introduced a new innovation called the 'three-generation mortgage'. Instead of the standard twenty-five-year mortgages available in places like the UK, these loans were to be repaid over periods of up to a hundred years. Taking on a mortgage is a tough enough decision as it is, but many Japanese were now taking out a loan that not only they would be responsible for but also their children and their grandchildren. To many outsiders (and unborn grandchildren!) this seemed like madness. But judging by how Japanese people were investing their money at

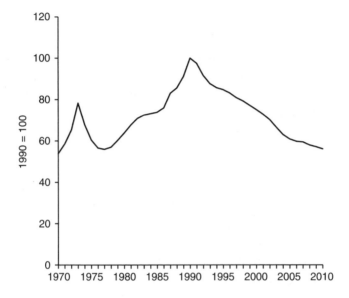

**Figure 8.1.** Real house prices in Japan, 1970–2010.
*Data source*: OECD.[3]

the time, many expected economic growth rates to continue at around 8% per year.[4]

Of course, this was not the case. In fact, 8% turned out to be ten times too optimistic. After having outpaced the rest of the world, Japan's economy slumped to an average real growth rate of just 0.8%. To contain the rapid rise in land prices the Bank of Japan had raised interest rates and the government had begun to introduce limits on bank lending to property companies. The policy of restricted lending did not last long, but by the time it was revoked the damage had already been done.[5]

By August 1992 average stock prices had fallen 60% from their 1989 peak. House prices, meanwhile, fell as if from the top of a rollercoaster, as shown in figure 8.1. The height from which they descended provided the momentum and since 1990 they have lost around 45% of their peak real value. Millions of homebuyers suffered substantial losses on the largest purchases of their lives, and the banks that had lent to them lost tens of trillions of yen.[6] The government was forced to bail out the economy with a far-reaching government spending programme and interest rates were slashed to zero. But Japan's growth was so slow that prices across the whole economy began to drop. The resulting deflation only worked to extend the period of miserable economic growth all the way up to the present day.

The warning that Japan offers is not just for heads of government or economic policymakers, however: it extends to ordinary people and particularly homeowners. If a crisis could hit one of the world's economic stars, it could hit anywhere. Two places where Japan's cautionary tale will resonate most loudly are in the corners of Europe: Ireland and Spain. In the twenty years that Japan has been standing stone still, these countries have been on an entirely different journey, but one that is in danger of leading to the same destination.

## CELTIC TIGER, HIDDEN DANGERS

Throughout the 1970s and 1980s, Ireland's economy had been stuck in a rut. The country had high unemployment, draining levels of emigration and sapping government debt.[7]

Ireland was one of the poorest countries in Western Europe and unemployment had been around 15% for much of the 1980s. Yet by the early 1990s this was slowly, and invisibly, changing. After several failed attempts, the government began to tackle its debt problems with tough controls on spending, it started brokering wage reductions with the unions and had successfully devalued the currency. With financial support from the European Union of around 3% of its GDP, Ireland was able to invest in much-needed education and infrastructure. Put together, these reforms worked to improve the country's competitiveness, launching an explosion in exports that would see the country catch up with, and then overtake, the average standard of living in Europe.

From 1995 to 2000, Ireland's economy grew by more than 10% each year. For the first time in the country's modern history it was at full employment. People were no longer leaving Ireland to find their fortune – people were arriving in droves. The only other countries that could match Ireland's economic performance at the time were in Southeast Asia: the so-called Asian tigers. Ireland took its place in this exclusive club, being dubbed the 'Celtic Tiger'.

By 2000, real house prices had risen to about two-and-a-half times their 1980s values, rising at nearly 8% each year during the 1990s. The chief causes were higher incomes and growing immigration, particularly from Eastern Europe. But by the turn of the millennium, Ireland had caught up with core EU members; its previously cheap labour force began demanding higher wages, in part to pay for, among other things, the pricier housing.

When Ireland joined ten other members of the EU in founding the euro in 1999, however, an opportunity for a new round of rapid growth presented itself. As a condition of joining Europe's single currency, Ireland had to surrender the right to set its own interest rate to the European Central Bank, which would instead set a central interest rate to target low inflation across all member countries. This meant that the interest rate for booming Ireland and other countries on the edge of Europe was the same as that for the established, mature economies that were growing at a steadier pace, such as Germany. This provided the already fast-growing Ireland with access to more credit at even cheaper levels than before. If Ireland's first wave of growth was built on the foundation of sound economics, the next wave was built on the foundation of property – and you can already guess where the story is heading.

The Irish went from making money by selling to Europe to making money by selling houses – to each other. In the 1990s, Ireland generated about 5% of its national income from house building – the usual level for a developed economy; by 2007 that figure was 15%.[8]

Ireland had never experienced a property crash to caution the collective consciousness and its banks started to believe their own hype, lending 40% more to property developers in 2008 than they had lent to everyone in Ireland in 2000.[9] Over that period home ownership reached one of the highest levels in the world at between 80% and 90%.[10] Economic growth continued to average 6% each year and house prices, already high, increased by another 50% in real terms between 2000 and 2006. In fifteen years real house prices in Ireland had trebled in value.[11]

## THE SAME IN SPAIN

Joining Ireland's property party was Spain. Having entered the European Union in 1986, ten years after Ireland did, it too had a tough past to overcome to reach the standard of living in central and northern Europe. The country's young democracy was still in its nursery years, having emerged from forty years of dictatorship and escaped a coup attempt barely four years earlier, yet Spain soon thrived with its all-access pass to a richer club. At the turn of the millennium the Spanish economy was in a rude state of health and had been growing steadily since the early 1990s. Its population had swelled due to immigration, particularly from Spanish-speaking South America. Between 1998 and 2008 the number of working-age people rose by close to 20%, with some economists believing that this put short-term pressure on house prices, which rose rapidly over this period.[12]

In 1999 Spain joined Ireland as a founding member of the euro and, like Ireland, began to reap the rewards from an interest rate that was accommodating the slowcoaches of Europe. With higher inflation in Spain than in Germany, the *real* interest rates Spaniards were paying on their borrowing – that is, nominal interest rates minus inflation – were much lower. According to the Bank of Spain, real interest rates were at their lowest level since 1990.[13] Suddenly Spaniards, like the Irish, could borrow at much cheaper rates.

The banks helped make things even easier for borrowers by competing ferociously for mortgages. Signing up a mortgage customer meant getting a customer for life, so the theory went, and the near-zero gains made on mortgages could be compensated by commissions on other services such as pensions. The personal debt of Spaniards rocketed. Real house prices, which had fallen in the early 1990s, started to rise in 1997 and nearly doubled between 2000 and 2006.

Many Spaniards were getting rich. During the 2000s Spain was creating one in every three jobs in the euro area[14] and in the years just after 2002 one in every four €500 notes in Europe was on Spanish soil.[15] At the height of the boom, in 2006, banks had a total of €544 billion on loan to homebuyers – and during that year more houses were built in Spain than were built in the UK, France and Germany combined.[16] As prices rose, many wished to buy a second home – either as a holiday home or to rent out – before prices rose further.

Of course, the boom would not be complete without government playing its part. Since the 1980s, the Spanish government had been subsidizing home ownership at a cost of around $15 billion – or 1% of the country's economic output – each year. One of the government's measures allowed homeowners to deduct 15% of their mortgage payments from their income taxes – a policy that was only removed in 2011.[17] From 1981 to 2010, home ownership in Spain rose from 22% to 86% – joining Ireland with one of the highest levels in the world.[18]

House prices were rising at a dizzying rate, fast enough to rival anywhere in the world. It seemed unsustainable and, to many, like pure speculation. In Spain, the vast majority of borrowers have variable-interest-rate mortgages. Add to this the high amounts of debt people had got into to buy property and Spain was in dangerous territory. But many did not seem to care. In 2005, José García-Montalvo, an economics professor at Pompeu Fabra University in Barcelona, surveyed thousands of new Spanish homeowners. He found that 95% of respondents felt they had bought an overvalued house, but when the same people were asked where they expected prices to go in the next few years, they forecasted double-digit percentage growth rates.[19] Their beliefs seemed flawed: if something is overvalued, how can you expect the price to grow? In fact, their reasoning was deliciously simple: buy quickly, get rich and get out before the party is over.

## HAUNTED HOUSES

By 2008, Europe's property party was indeed over. Shares in Ireland's three main banks crashed: having lent an amount equal to two-thirds of the value of the country's entire economy to property developers, often without collateral, the market had lost confidence in them.[20] When Ireland's house prices peaked in 2006, and the number of unsold housing units began to reach alarming levels, these banks fell into serious trouble. By 2008 the Irish government would be forced to improvise a series of desperate and expensive responses, including guaranteeing the banking sector.

Just thirty-five kilometres to the south of Madrid is the town of Sesena. Designed as a satellite town from which people can commute to the capital, it overwhelms the arid landscape: a new development of 14,000 apartment blocks, sitting by the road like giant cubes of red brick. Today, with Spain's housing market in a rut, many thousands of the flats remain empty. The shops that were promised remain half built and many that were finished are boarded up. This is one of Spain's many ghost towns with a twist: here, the residents did not leave, they never arrived. More examples are to be found just a short distance from Madrid and the other main cities. Ten kilometres north of Madrid's centre is Las Tablas; fifty kilometres to the northeast is Yebes. The Bank of Spain estimates that across the whole of the country, around a million properties remain unsold – one for every forty-five people.

## PROPERTY MANIA

Ireland too has a huge stockpile of empty houses – also given the eerie title of ghost estates – with around 300,000 vacant properties or abandoned houses in a country with a population of just 4.5 million.[21]

One person who saw this coming was Morgan Kelly, an economic historian at University College Dublin. In 2007 Kelly wrote the provocatively titled paper, 'On the likely extent of falls in Irish house prices', claiming that the boom was unsustainable and predicting a fall of 40–60% in house prices over the next eight or nine years.[22] At that time Kelly was called everything from an eccentric to a lunatic, even by people such as Ireland's Taoiseach, Bertie Ahern.

While some in Ireland knew that a property crash was imminent but chose to play along, many more actually believed in the investments they were making. One of the unique things about Ireland's banking crisis is that many of the senior figures at the failed banks are themselves bankrupt, in stark contrast with former bankers in the US and elsewhere. Though it was gloomy, Kelly's prediction was outstandingly accurate: house prices soon crashed, falling by nearly 40% in nominal and real terms between the peak and the end of 2010, as shown in figure 8.2. Kelly is now referred to as the sage of the Irish housing market.

Ireland was in no state to cope with the chaos it had created. On top of the banking crisis was the loss in wage competitiveness that had been getting steadily worse since 2000 and fragile government finances that were heavily dependent on a continuation of the boom. The country has since received an €85 billion bailout package from the European Union and the International Monetary Fund as it tries to pull its economy out of the mire. Ireland's property boom and the resultant losses have bankrupted the country.

### GETTING TO THE BOTTOM OF THIS

In the heart of Dublin, looming over some of the city's most luxurious shopping arcades and splendid gardens, stands the landmark Shelbourne Hotel. Founded in 1824, the hotel's main claim

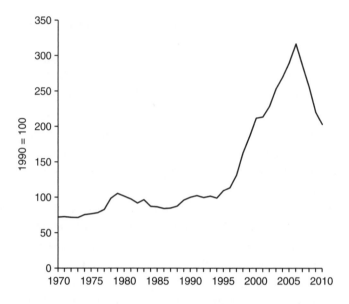

**Figure 8.2.** Real house prices in Ireland, 1970–2010.
*Data source*: OECD.

to historical fame came in 1922 when the Irish Constitution was drafted in its room 112. Yet it is a far less inspiring, and far more recent, meeting within its walls that offers a glimpse of what is happening in Ireland's property market today.

Three hundred and fifty people crowded into its grand Gatsby-like conference suites to participate in one of the largest ever auctions of Irish property. Even at the start over a hundred people stood outside relaying their bids to the auctioneers. With the hustle and bustle of buying and selling echoing around the building's high ceilings, you could be forgiven for thinking this was a sign of a booming Irish housing market. But this was April 2011 and at that sitting properties were selling at around one-third of their peak prices of just four years earlier. A four-bedroom mews house in the upmarket Ballsbridge area of Dublin sold for €550,000 – at its peak it had been valued at around €2 million. Back in 2007 apartments in a development in Castleknock, Dublin were being sold for €565,000 for two-bedroom units and €750,000 for

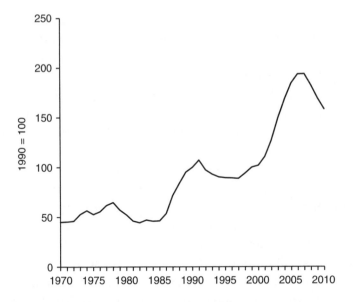

**Figure 8.3.** Real house prices in Spain, 1970–2010.
*Data source*: OECD.

three-bedroom ones. Now the two-bedroom flats were going for
€160,000 and the three-bedroom ones for around €200,000. While
the new owners beamed in delight, it seems unlikely that many
of the old owners shared their enthusiasm.

By the end of that day eighty-one properties had been sold,
raising €15 million. The cheapest sold for €22,500 and the most
expensive for €600,000. But these prices were not only a very long
way below the values of 2006, they were also well below the values at which equivalent properties were being marketed by estate
agents – and therefore the value that official house price indices
had been using. Prices in Dublin had collapsed, but instead of
selling at a loss, many sellers were staying put and buyers were
keeping their wallets firmly closed. The volume of sales had plummeted, meaning that an accurate measure of house prices was
hard to come by – indeed, one house price index even stopped
providing monthly reports because there were too few transactions for the results to be representative. That is why the auction

was of such national interest. Here was a real sense of the market price. Here demand was literally meeting supply, and it was not a pretty sight for most homeowners. According to this measure, house prices were down by well over 60%.

Over in Spain, the central bank has reported that official house prices have fallen by 17% since 2007 – a much smaller fall than that seen in Ireland. This fall is reflected in the house price data in figure 8.3. Yet some experts, including Professor García-Montalvo, suggest that we treat these numbers with caution. The 17% drop that the Bank of Spain quotes is based on house valuation appraisals from property companies (many of which are owned by banks) and not on transactions, as they are elsewhere in this book. As many disgruntled people selling their houses in recent years will remind you – especially those in the Shelbourne Hotel – there is a big difference between the two valuation methods. One reason why Spain relies on this measure is that at the time of setting up the index in the mid 1980s, many houses were still being bought and sold on the black market, meaning that setting up a reliable house price index would have been too costly.

Some observers believe that the fall in transaction values in Spain has been much steeper than reported in the official figures. Estate agents say that prices of homes have typically fallen by between 20% and 50%, with no part of the country spared. But this raises the question of why anyone would want to downplay the fall? Most people agree that there are around one million empty properties in Spain, meaning that the market will suffer from oversupply for several years. Moreover, the chances of inflation eroding real prices are slim. Spain may have benefited from being part of the euro for much of the last ten years, but now the region's commitment to low inflation is likely to make Spain's housing market correction more painful. This suggests there is only one way prices can go – and if they get there too quickly, it will be disastrous for Spain's banks and, many would argue, the economy too.

For this reason, García-Montalvo and other economists like him think that house prices in Spain will readjust slowly. Banks will be less likely to sell the properties they have acquired, will be less likely to force others to sell and, some argue, less likely to encourage property companies to lower their valuations. If they are right, house prices in Spain will be falling in real and nominal terms for much of the next decade – if not longer.

In Ireland, meanwhile, data from the Irish bank Permanent TSB suggests that at the end of 2010 the average price of a house in Ireland was €190,000, compared with around €215,000 in 2009 and €311,000 at the peak in 2006 – an overall fall of 38%.[23] According to Morgan Kelly, a stable level for Ireland's house prices (one that is in line with sustainable levels of lending and borrowing) is around two-thirds below the peak: the level reached in the Shelbourne Hotel auction, and the level prices were at in the late 1990s. With prices falling at around 12% each year, it will be 2015 or 2016 before prices reach this level.*

## AN UNFINISHED STORY

We cannot be sure how the stories in Ireland and Spain will pan out. In Ireland, the government's ability to finance its debt is dependent on the support of the European Union and the International Monetary Fund, and many even question whether this support will be enough. Such are the parallels between the two countries that Spain has to continuously deny that it is about to receive the same treatment. For both countries it is certain that government cuts will be a drag on economic growth for some years to come.

Whatever the final extent of the fall, we already know that the values ascribed to houses at the height of the boom were illusory. The creation and destruction of wealth is almost beyond comprehension: in Ireland, the value of housing is estimated to have increased from around €100 billion in 1997 to a peak value of

*Average prices are €190,000 as of Q4 2010. Down 12% from €215,000 in Q4 2009. Prices are down 38% from 2006 peak of €311,000. If prices fall 66% from their peak, they have another €90,000 to fall to reach the levels Kelly suggests.

nearly €500 billion in 2007. Since the peak it has fallen by €150 billion according to the index and by €300 billion according to the latest auction data. By comparison, the entire GDP of Ireland is below €170 billion.

As we have seen elsewhere, the price expansion machine worked equally well in reverse. As prices fell, the apparent demand for houses evaporated. Credit availability disappeared. But the houses and the building programme were still there. Prices started to fall, causing speculative demand to fall further. Homeowners, many with negative equity, could not or would not move and so transactions dried up. Today these housing markets are composed of mainly those people who need to buy or sell, and it will take some time before we know at what new level prices will settle.

In Spain, however, the crisis has at least presented some opportunities. We can see a side-effect of rising house prices and home ownership over the last few decades in what it does to the rest of the economy. If the majority of people own houses and house prices are high, then while that may be a good thing for those staying in their homes, those looking to move face fewer options. With such an underdeveloped rental market in Spain, the only viable option for many people has been to buy – but the cost of buying a house every time you move prevents people from moving from city to city in search of work. This is one of the reasons why Spain's unemployment has been so high. In 2010 unemployment nationally was around 20% – the highest in Europe – but while it was around 30% in the south it was only 10% in the north.[24]

The Spanish government is taking steps to rectify this by removing some of the tax benefits for home ownership and by encouraging growth in the number of rental properties – something that a lot more homeowners are likely to consider in an attempt to recover some of their lost investment. Spain hopes to have levels of rental closer to the European average of 30% by 2020, compared with their current level of just over 10% today. The government has understood that it makes no sense to continue to promote home ownership.

Back in Ireland, the country's central bank highlights the extent of the failure of bank management and of a government that had created and supported, in its own words, 'a credit-fuelled property market and construction frenzy' and nurtured the widespread notion that 'the party could last forever'.[25] Morgan Kelly is even more frank about Ireland's journey since 1990: 'from basket case to superstar and back again'.[26]

## POSSIBLE ENDINGS

Ireland and Spain have seen similar patterns in their housing markets, as their fast-growth economies became turbo-charged with plentiful cheap debt. Extensive and unnecessary construction did little to slow the speculation on the way up and is very likely to be a drag on the recovery on the way down. Our lessons from housing markets over long time periods is that the markets will probably return to their previous norms, but we have also seen that the amount of time this takes can vary from a few years to many decades. While there are warnings that these countries could follow the same plot line as Japan, there is another story that started at the same time as the Japanese house price boom but had a different ending: we turn now to Sweden.

Like Japan, Sweden's financial markets were deregulated during the 1980s, leading to fierce competition for customers and an apparent race to see who could provide the riskiest loans. An asset bubble ensued, with stock prices growing three times faster than the world average throughout the decade and property prices rising by around 40% in real terms from 1985 to 1989.[27] But the high levels of demand eventually resulted in high inflation and wage increases. Banks – and then the economy more generally – fell into serious trouble. Three-quarters of the forty or so real estate companies listed on the Stockholm Stock Exchange during the 1980s had to be restructured or simply allowed to go bankrupt.[28] For both Japan and Sweden the peak was in 1989, but unlike the dire picture in Japan, Sweden had returned to normal within five years.

Sweden's government introduced a bank guarantee that protected all creditors, apart from shareholders, against loss, and Swedish authorities encouraged the greatest possible openness about the financial situations of the banks they were supporting. This meant banks recognizing their losses, often in property.

The crisis in Sweden was painful but it was brief. By 1995 the economy was back to normal, with house prices having lost all of their earlier gains. The contrast with Japan is striking. Some even argue that the bottom of Japan's property slump is yet to be reached, so high were prices in the 1980s and so reluctant have the banks been to come clean about their losses, with the result that bank lending and economic recovery keep being pushed back. Japan's bust held down the economy for twenty years, partly because of policy failures but in large part because of the size of the bubble that preceded it. While Japan started to recover in the 2000s, it has not been immune from the global financial crisis. Exactly twenty years after its peak, the Nikkei was still at barely one-quarter of the level of its previous value.[29] Meanwhile, real house prices are still 45% below their 1990 peak.

Sweden's boom and bust was relatively fast. The challenges for Ireland and Spain are perhaps even more severe, given the level of overvaluation, the weakness of the banks' and the government's balance sheets and, as members of the euro area, the inability to use inflation to whittle down real debt. Even more ominously, Japan's real house prices peaked at 80% above their pre-boom levels, in Ireland it was over 200% and in Spain it was 120%.* The path to stability in these countries may be long and painful.

## WORDS OF WARNING

The catastrophic trilogy of earthquake, tsunami and nuclear meltdown in Japan in early 2011 remind us that there are much more important things than bricks and mortar. That it should affect an

---

*Japan 1977 to peak in 1990; Ireland 1994 to peak in 2006; Spain 1997 to peak in 2007.

economy still in the recovery position is all the more devastating. The recent disasters aside, there is plenty about Japan's story to make homeowners nervous – wherever in the world they may be.

Japan's story seems to defy some of the normal explanations for a housing slump. Japan has roughly the same area as Germany but it has 50% more people living in it. Its population density is more than three times that of Spain and nearly six times that of Ireland. Interest rates are effectively zero. These are all things that we might think would contribute to keeping prices high.

Japan is no longer the most expensive market in the world. To some observers it is cheap, with more than a few saying that now is the ideal time to buy in Japan. The bad times cannot last forever, they argue. But as we have seen in other countries in this book, there is no reason why they cannot last for a lot longer than they have so far.

# CHAPTER 9

---

# THE HISTORICAL PICTURE

FOR MOST OF THE LAST four hundred years, if you owned a house along the Herengracht Canal in Amsterdam you would have seen very modest growth in the real value of your home. For most of the last hundred years the same would have been true if you had owned a house in the US, Australia and Norway. In France, the last century saw house prices collapse in the first half and then rebound in the second, and the records suggests, at least tentatively, that sustained substantial real house price increases have been a rarity over the last six hundred years. For most of the people who lived during the last few centuries, the idea that your home could be a source of great wealth would have been dismissed as a fantasy.

Yet in the UK, our experience over our lifetimes has been of rising house prices, albeit with occasional dips lasting only a few years before the upward trend re-emerges. We find it difficult to picture the effects of inflation, to adjust for compounding or to disentangle the effect of mortgage leverage – all of which make us prone to overestimate the attractiveness of housing as an investment. But even when we take these factors into account, our experience has been that real house prices rise steadily.

This contrast with other countries should cause us to question whether our beliefs will continue to be reinforced for the next thirty or forty years.

Another clear message that stands out is that predicting short-term movements in the housing market is difficult, if not impossible.* We have seen long periods in which the market has seemed slow to respond to changing economic events and we have seen periods in which it has appeared to overreact. What we can do is use what we have seen in this book to try to explain the longer-term movements. To do this, let us look back at the period from 1900 to 2010 for the five countries that we have examined so far: the US, Norway, Australia, the Netherlands and France. Not only is this the time frame within which our indices are most accurate, it is also a period of widespread change that can help us identify some of the key drivers of house price movements.

Figure 9.1 shows a simple average of the data from the five countries along with the trends for each. We can see some broad patterns: most countries saw flat house prices before the First World War; house prices fell between the First and Second World Wars; house prices then rose gently from the 1940s until the turn of the millennium and then, in most countries, shot up in the last decade.

But beneath this average are some significant variations. As the First World War broke out, it was a difficult time for house prices, as for so much else. War and the subsequent economic difficulties in the 1920s and 1930s shook France particularly badly – something only made worse by the government's stringent rent controls. House prices in Australia and Norway, meanwhile, were somewhat less affected by war, for obvious reasons.

Following the Second World War, real prices across the five countries rose at an average yearly rate of 1.7% between 1946 and 1995. Looking at countries individually, French house prices

*Even experts get this wrong. In May 2003 *The Economist* ran a feature article entitled 'Castles in hot air: is another bubble about to burst?', arguing that house prices were overvalued (by 30% in the UK, for example). Over the next four years UK house prices rose by nearly 20% in real terms.

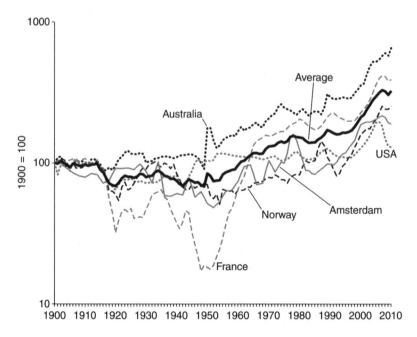

**Figure 9.1.** House price indices across five countries, 1900–2010 (logarithmic scale).

*Data sources*: as previously noted for each separate country.

rebounded from their terrible prewar performance to grow at 4.2% per year, which might simply have been because they were catching up to a normal price level after decades of regulation, controls and economic woes. Australian house prices grew at a healthy 2.0% each year, although the early part of this was also a rebound from wartime rent and price controls. House prices in Norway grew at 0.8% per year, those in Amsterdam at 1.5% per year, while those in the US barely grew at all, with prices effectively flat. During this long period of increasing prosperity the average growth in real house prices was around 1.7% each year.

In the last fifteen years, real house prices across all the countries have risen at an average rate of 4.7% annually. The rates in Australia and Norway are around 6%, while US house prices also rose at over 6% per year until 2006 before giving up almost all of those gains. Amsterdam and France have seen annual gains of 3.2% and 4.6% respectively. This strong performance across so many countries is unprecedented.

To get a sense of how rare it has been to have such high growth in prices, we can look at the distribution of price increases over the whole 110-year period. Because the typical amount of time a homeowner stays in their house before moving is about ten years, figure 9.2 shows how much house prices change over that amount of time. We start with the change from 1900 to 1910, then from 1901 to 1911, and so on until 2000–2010. Across the five countries there are 505 such periods.

Across these 505 ten-year periods, the average yearly increase is 1.0% in real terms, while the median is 0.7%. In nearly a sixth of the periods, real house prices fall by more than 2% annually. In just over a fifth they fall by between 0% and 2%. This means that for a total of 37% of the time, real prices fall for ten years or more. In just under a fifth of cases real house prices increase modestly at between 0% and 1%. In just over a fifth of cases, prices increase by between 1% and 3%, and in just a fifth of cases the rises are above 3%. So while the average is an increase of around 1%, there is a great deal of variation even over decade-long periods.

In the worst 10% of the periods studied, real house values fell by more than a quarter in ten years (a loss of more than 3% each year).* Producing such substantial negative returns appears to require dramatic events: wars, draconian regulation, major recessions or major bubbles bursting. The losses we are seeing in some markets now, such as those in the US or Ireland, are of this order or even greater.

There were 109 periods in which prices rose by more than a third over the course of a decade (a gain of over 3% each year for

*Slightly more than 50 of the 505 periods examined had such a fall. Twenty-one were around the First World War and the recessions that followed; five were in Amsterdam before the Second World War; thirteen were in France from the Second World War onwards, continuing until the early 1950s; six were in Norway in the 1950s; and six were in Amsterdam in the late 1980s.

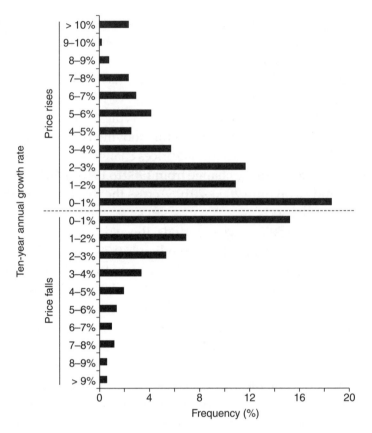

**Figure 9.2.** Distribution of annual real increases in house prices over ten-year periods.

a decade).* Nearly half of these have occurred since 1995, again reinforcing how unusual recent times have been for house prices across many countries.

As we survey all the data and the history, the picture that emerges is that real house prices have increased at fairly modest rates, averaging 1% each year over the five countries and the

---

*Nearly half of these 109 periods (47) have occurred since 1995 across the five countries; nineteen (and all the very largest increases) occurred in France after the Second World War as the market recovered; the rest are spread around as transient booms occurred in different countries.

110 years between 1900 and 2010. But within this there have been considerable swings, particularly in the last couple of decades, with prices rising at a rate of 5–10%. This raises the question of whether we should set our expectations for future changes in UK house prices closer to the modest historical level across the countries studied. Or should we set our expectations closer to the rapid rise of recent years?


## NOT EVERYONE CAME TO THE PARTY

As we saw in Germany, the unprecedented rise in prices over the last fifteen years has not been matched everywhere. As well as looking back over hundreds of years, we can also look at how house prices have performed more recently, and thanks to data provided by the OECD, we are able to do this for a wider range of countries. Using 1990 as a starting point we can split countries into those in which there has been virtually no increase over the last twenty years, those in which prices have almost doubled and those in which they have more than doubled (or at least had done, at their peak).

In Germany, Switzerland, Japan, Finland and Italy real house prices have been broadly flat, as shown in figure 9.3.* In fact, in Germany, Switzerland and Japan house prices have trended down, seemingly oblivious to the boom taking place elsewhere. Identifying the reason for this is not straightforward. We all know that Japan has had very, very low interest rates, but that has not been sufficient to cause a boom. We all know that Germany is a hugely successful economy, but that has not caused a boom. We all know that Switzerland has great wealth, and yet that has not caused a boom. Taken together, then, this evidence does not seem to point to a single, global explanation of why house prices boom.

---

*To ensure consistency across a large number of countries, the data for house prices in this chapter comes from the OECD.

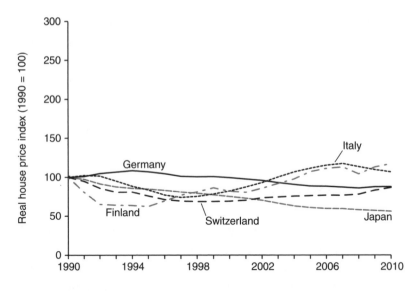

**Figure 9.3.** Countries where real prices were flat.
*Data source*: OECD.[1]

In the US, France, Canada, Sweden and Spain prices nearly doubled between 1990 and their peak, as shown in figure 9.4. If we look at the US, we know that for a very long time real house prices were flat, and yet they rose rapidly over this recent period. We also know that they are now falling back. Yet while US house prices have jumped only to come crashing back down, population growth has been steadily rising (as it has for the last two centuries), economic growth was no better than during the other postwar decades, real wages, if anything, grew more slowly than in the past, and the availability of land and rates of construction have not changed much either.

The most likely cause of the historic rise is a change in people's beliefs about house prices. This belief extended to the banks that were providing the loans. In the US, more generous mortgages meant that millions of people who would not previously have been able to buy a house were now able to do so.

In Spain we have seen that a huge construction boom that created an enormous increase in supply did not slow price growth.

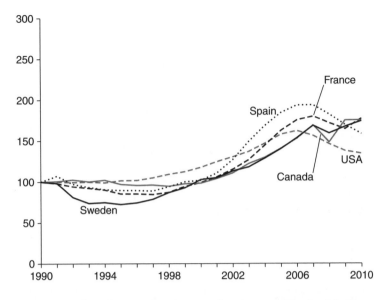

**Figure 9.4.** Countries where real prices nearly doubled.

As we have seen, some houses were bought as second homes and many remain empty. Again, the likely cause seems to have been the expansion in credit coupled with low interest rates, unleashing a previously dormant demand for houses.

In some countries the increase in house prices was even more dramatic, as shown in figure 9.5. Ireland led the pack on the way up – and it is leading the pack on the way down. There, real house prices tripled to their peak in 2006. They have already lost half of that increase and, if they fall as far as the auction data we have looked at suggests they will, they will eventually give up all of the rise. With Ireland's beleaguered government facing high interest rates and credit restrictions, it has been unable to prop up the housing market.

The resource-rich countries of Australia and Norway have yet to see their markets decline. With huge balance-of-payments surpluses, liquidity in their financial systems is very strong, and interest rates are very low. These countries do not need to rebalance their books for the time being. We may not know for some years

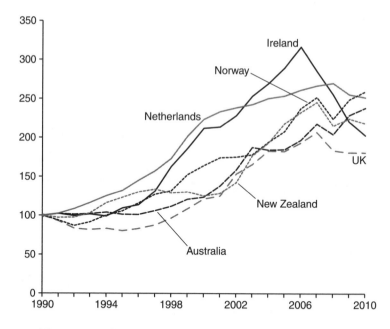

**Figure 9.5.** Countries where prices more than doubled.

whether Australia and Norway will follow the US and Ireland or whether they will provide a different story as to how house prices can evolve.

The Netherlands is in a more precarious position. Its house prices have increased at about double the rate of those in the US, and, while prices have fallen a little, the falls have been minor in comparison with those in Ireland and the US. One reason for this might be the constraints on supply that added to the boom, but as we have seen elsewhere, the larger part of the increase appears to have been due to an increase in demand facilitated by mortgage availability and low interest rates. The Netherlands is joined by Australia, Canada and Norway in a group of countries where prices have fallen by just a little, or not at all.

The next few years will see one of two things. Either we will see a substantial reversion in real prices across many of the countries we have looked at or, if some countries maintain their high real price levels, we will see a new paradigm for house prices –

something quite different from anything we have seen over the last few centuries. To explore how the future might evolve we need to delve deeper into the causes of the recent surge.


## THE BUILDING BLOCKS OF HOUSE PRICES

As you will have noted, there is no simple story, no single reason why house prices have boomed in some countries over the last twenty years while remaining flat in others. Table 9.1 lists OECD countries according to the size of the rise in house prices in them between 1990 and 2007. The countries with the largest increases tend to have had slightly higher rates of population growth and a stronger rise in mortgage debt. In some of these countries there has been extensive construction – often well ahead of population growth. In countries where house price rises have been more modest, population growth has tended to be lower and mortgage debt has also grown by less.

Despite the apparent correlation between population growth and rises in house prices, we have seen in this book that this does not hold in the long run: supply has always adjusted eventually. This might suggest that mortgage debt is the main factor, and, since mortgage debt in many countries has reached an unprecedented level, we are unsure how much further it can continue to grow. But before we draw any firm conclusions, let us look back at the lessons we can draw from our exploration of house prices throughout history.


## THE COST OF BUILDING A HOUSE

Perhaps the first question to ask is, how was it possible for house prices in some countries to have been close to flat for so many decades? At first this seems very counterintuitive. But it might seem less peculiar if we consider what makes up the value of a house. Breaking it down, a house is a plot of land (usually quite a

**Table 9.1.** House prices, 1990–2010.

| | Real house price change (%) | | Population change (%) | Increase in number of houses (%) | Mortgage debt as percentage of GDP | |
|---|---|---|---|---|---|---|
| | 1990–2007 | 2007–2010 | 1998–2010 | 1998–2010 | 1998 | 2009 |
| Ireland | 185 | −29 | 20 | 47 | 26 | 90 |
| Netherlands | 167 | −6 | 5 | 10 | 55 | 106 |
| Norway | 152 | 3 | 9 | 13 | 40 | 71 |
| New Zealand | 146 | −11 | 17 | 18 | 54 | 89 |
| Australia | 118 | 9 | 16 | 20 | 38 | 86 |
| UK | 107 | −13 | 6 | 9* | 50 | 88 |
| Spain | 94 | −18 | 16 | 38 | 24 | 65 |
| France | 80 | −2 | 7 | 14* | 20 | 38 |
| Canada | 69 | 4 | 10 | 15 | 45 | 58 |
| Sweden | 69 | 3 | 5 | 6 | 44 | 82 |
| US | 56 | −14 | 11 | 11 | 54 | 81 |
| Italy | 17 | −9 | 6 | n.a. | 8 | 22 |
| Finland | 13 | 4 | 3 | 13 | 30 | 58 |
| Germany | −13 | 1 | 0 | 7 | 52 | 48 |
| Switzerland | −23 | 13 | 5 | 14 | — | 102 |
| Japan | −41 | −7 | 1 | 15 | 34 | 37 |

*Data sources*: OECD; EMF; World Bank; ONS. *Data is to 2007 rather than to 2010.

small plot), some materials (bricks, glass, wires and the like) and many hours of labour from different trades.

To understand how these all come together, we can call on an excellent resource: Mark Brinkley's *Housebuilder's Bible*.[2] Brinkley points out that

> whilst material costs haven't changed that much in the past fifteen years, labour rates have… In 1994 [bricklayers charged] £180 per thousand [bricks laid]. Today it varies between £300 per thousand … to over £500 per thousand.

Adjusting for inflation, the £180 labour cost from 1994 is equivalent to £280 in today's money, so the rise in the cost of labour in real terms is around 40% (or just above 2% per year). This annual increase is very much in line with how real wages have grown more generally. If material costs have been flat in nominal terms, that means they have fallen by about a third in real terms (a fall of about 3% per year), with the falls driven by increased productivity, improving technology and better sourcing of products.

The usual rule of thumb is that the cost of building a house, excluding land costs, is about half labour and half materials. So with falling material costs and rising labour costs this usually nets out so that total costs remain flat. Robert Shiller, whom we met in chapter 2 on the US, has made an estimate of real building costs in the US over the last 120 years showing that costs rose on average by 0.4% each year. A report by the UK government in 2004 estimated that construction costs across six countries increased at a typical real annual rate of 0.7% over the period 1991–2002.[3] So if the cost of land on which to build does not jump, it becomes easy to see how the cost of a like-for-like house could stay roughly the same over time.

This can help us understand why some countries have flat or hardly moving prices for long periods, while at the same time having growing populations, rising wages and thriving construction industries. If the fundamental cost of building houses only increases slowly, it raises the question of why house prices do not simply grow at a gentle 0.5–1% per year at all times. In fact, across the five countries for which we have examined the history of house prices since 1900, the actual increase has averaged 1% per year. It therefore seems a more reasonable 'base case' from which further increases or falls need to be explained.

### A SHORTAGE OF HOUSES?

One argument that has frequently been made at many times in many countries – including in Amsterdam over the centuries, in Norway during the growth of the main cities, in Australia today, and frequently in the UK – is that a permanent shortage of houses will lead to ever-increasing house prices.

In 2004 this argument led the then UK government to ask economist Kate Barker to produce a report examining the housing market and the balance of demand and supply. Put simply, the report argued that the number of households in the UK was outgrowing the number of houses for them to live in. With demand outstripping supply, houses were bound to become even more unaffordable for many.

One view is that there is insufficient land, but it is clear that this is not the problem: rather, there is an unwillingness to use the available land to build houses. A recent article observed that only about 10% of England is urbanized, and an even smaller proportion of Britain.[4] The current conversion of land to urban use is minimal. Moreover, the UK has a population density of around 240 people per square kilometre, which is similar to the level in Germany – a country with a much less overinflated housing market, as we have seen.

Another view is that population growth has put unbearable pressure on supply. Again, this argument does not by itself hold up. The US, Amsterdam, Norway, France and Australia have all experienced substantial population growth since 1900 and this has not led to a continuous surge in house prices. While it is true in the UK that the population has roughly doubled, from around thirty million in 1900 to around sixty million today, the number of houses has more than trebled. These extra houses have been needed: falling family sizes mean that fewer people are living in one house, immigration has exceeded emigration, and people now live longer.

The Barker review took the view that in order for real house prices to rise at the then EU average of 1.1% per year, England alone needed to build an extra 120,000 private-sector houses in addition to the 130,000 or so that were being built at that time. In fact, house building did rise to around 170,000 houses per year by 2006–7, but these extra 40,000 houses did not lead to a slowdown in house prices. Instead, real price increases actually jumped to

5–10% each year rather than the historical level the report was aiming for. This suggests, once again, that there is more to the price rises than just a physical shortage of supply.

## SHORT-TERM SHOCKS TO THE SYSTEM

Another pattern we have seen is for house prices to rise for a few years before falling back to their earlier levels (or vice versa). These cycles seem to occur for a variety of reasons but the key feature is that the market eventually adapts and normality returns.

We have seen prices increase when there is a surge in the population, only for prices to fall back again once housing supply responds. This has happened many times, including in seventeenth-century Amsterdam, nineteenth-century Oslo and Australia during the gold rush. In the opposite direction, the influenza pandemic after the First World War, the various plagues during Amsterdam's long history and the emigration from Norway to the US in the late nineteenth century all decreased prices until population growth returned.[5]

One unexpected cycle seems to occur when there is strong inflation or deflation. During times of high inflation, the real price of a house can fall substantially for no reason other than the fact that the prices of other things has risen in relative terms. During wartime, the rationing of goods drives up their prices and the inflation erodes the real value of a house. The same thing happens during resource scares such as the 1970s oil crisis. In the opposite direction, deflation can actually mean that the real price of a house rises, as happened in Norway after the Napoleonic Wars, for example. Because houses are traded less frequently than other things, the prices of other goods can inflate or deflate faster than house prices, meaning that by just standing still the real prices of houses can quickly change. These shocks only last as long as the inflation or deflation that caused them – but, as we have seen, these periods can last several years.

## REGULATION CAN HOLD PRICES DOWN
## (FOR A WHILE)

At various times in the countries we have looked at, governments have decided to step in and regulate price increases. Perhaps the most striking example of this was in France between the First World War and the 1950s: a period during which rent controls meant that houses were a very bad investment and house prices fell to less than half of their previous levels.

There have also been other, shorter, periods when government regulation has restrained prices. Australia regulated house prices directly between 1942 and 1949, causing many transactions to occur in increasingly convoluted ways to circumvent the system. In all of the countries we have looked at, when controls ended, house prices jumped.

Governments can also provide tax benefits and subsidies, as we have seen recently in Australia and Spain. But governments do not need to implement direct controls to have a major effect on prices. Through the regulation of banks and the mortgage market, and by control of the planning system, policymakers play a key role in determining house prices.

### PERIODS OF STRUCTURAL DECLINE

We have seen how house prices in most countries went into a severe decline between 1914 and the early 1920s. Before that they had been broadly flat, if a little volatile. But a string of events starting with the First World War, the subsequent flu pandemic and postwar recessions lowered population growth and living standards substantially. In addition, taxes to pay for the war further reduced disposable incomes, and as the Great Depression and the Second World War followed, house prices did not recover. Anyone who bought before 1914 would, in most countries, have had to wait until the 1950s or early 1960s before they were able to get their money back in real terms. France had a particularly weak property market due to a combination of these factors and the added weight of rent controls combined with inflation. In the US, house prices remained below their pre-First World War levels through the Roaring Twenties and, more understandably, through the depressed 1930s.

If we were to view that long period of decline as one in which house prices were below their normal level, it would mean that the subsequent recovery in the 1950s and 1960s was in large part prices returning to normal. An argument in favour of this can be found by looking again at our analysis of house building costs. Looking again at the whole period from 1900 to 1995 shows that real house price rises were minimal: overall, the real annual rise was 0.5% (1.1% in Australia, 0.7% in France, 0.1% in the US, 0% in Norway, 0.2% in Amsterdam). This very gentle long-term movement is consistent with how construction costs change and with the longer time series we have seen, particularly in Amsterdam.

If this interpretation is correct, it has a number of implications. First, it suggests that house prices can be blown off course by a series of extremely adverse events, possibly for some decades. Second, it reinforces the idea that the long-term evolution of house prices is usually a very slow increase driven by modestly rising costs. Third, it makes the more recent boom look even more exceptional.

### RECOVERIES, BOOMS AND BUBBLES

A further observation is that the housing market can be slow to readjust. After the Second World War the market did not bounce straight back to where it had been before the war, but rather took many years to slowly get back to normal. It was as if people's expectations of the value of houses, and therefore the prices at which they were willing to trade, adjusted slowly. There seems to be a memory effect, where recent history weighs heavily on our view of what is a high or a low price for a house. If this is true, it would explain the long time it took prices to recover from the lows of the 1920s and 1930s, and it may explain why price movements appear to show some momentum: we tend to see a price rise as confirmation that houses are a good investment and therefore we expect a further rise to be more likely.

Over our long journey we have seen a number of house price booms, where prices have increased much faster than the long-term average. Some of these episodes were caused by short-term shocks, as we have seen above, that then quickly reversed. But we have also seen a number of booms that have lasted much longer. Some booms might be seen as more permanent as they appear to have been caused by countries recovering from wars, severe recessions and other disasters that temporarily lowered prices below their normal levels. Others, particularly the most recent boom for those living in the US, the UK, France, the Netherlands, Australia, Spain, New Zealand, Canada, Norway and Ireland, raise the question of how long they will last.

As we look further into the past, there have been a number of booms that we can explore. We have seen house prices jump in Japan between 1977 and their peak in 1990, after which they have steadily declined back to their 1977 levels. This boom was driven by a mix of economic growth, financial deregulation and speculation, which affected other areas such as the stock market as well.

Amsterdam's long history has seen four long booms prior to the current one and in each case house prices reverted to trend, but only after many years. The 1660s saw house prices peak as the Dutch Republic reached its zenith; the next peak in the 1730s was during an economic boom based around the prospects for South American trade; industrialization led to the third boom in the 1880s; and a discovery of natural resources led to house prices booming in the late 1970s.

We have seen house prices increase in Paris between 1500 and 1800, but that was after two hundred years of decline. Another French boom that started in the mid 1850s was reversed when Napoleon III lost the Franco-Prussian war in 1871, and the modest boom around 1990 fell back to trend even more rapidly.

Our review of past booms leaves us with a clear picture: they tend to end with prices reverting back to trend. This reversion may take anything from one year to fifty years but the message from the history of house prices so far is that booms do not last forever.

### EXPLAINING THE RECENT BOOM

Population growth, increasing building costs, a shortage of supply, short-term shocks and fundamental changes in the economy all seem unable, by themselves, to explain why house prices in some countries have risen so fast for so long in recent years. It seems likely, then, that the rise was caused by a combination of factors – notably, people's beliefs that house prices will continue to rise, interest rates falling for the best part of a generation, and banks making mortgages readily available, sometimes even to those who had little prospect of ever repaying them out of earned income.[6]

Looking at the recent boom, house prices in several countries have already started to readjust back to trend – most notably in the US and Ireland. It would probably be unwise to bet against others following, but equally it would be unwise to bet on when that might happen.

### THERE ARE MANY DRIVERS OF REAL HOUSE PRICES

From what we have seen over hundreds of years of data, real house prices grow modestly over time: in line with the 0.5–1% level that we have seen over several countries over the last century or so. But house prices do diverge from this trend for a number of different reasons. Table 9.2 summarizes the main factors we have seen and notes a number of examples.

As we reflect on the broad range of experiences that we have seen – whether in the countries for which we have only forty or

**Table 9.2.** Drivers of real house prices.

| | Factors that tend to reduce house prices | Factors that tend to increase house prices |
|---|---|---|
| **Demographic** | • Depopulation (Japan 2000s)<br>• Emigration (Norway 1880s)<br>• Pandemics (1918 flu) | • Immigration (UK 2000s, Spain 1990s)<br>• Smaller household size (UK 1900–2010) |
| **Economic shocks** | • Slumps (Great Depression)<br>• Military defeat (France 1871) | • Natural resource discoveries (Netherlands 1970s, Australia 1880s, Norway 1970s) |
| **Supply of new houses** | • Supply growth/ overbuilding (Ireland and Spain 2000–2007) | • Limited construction (UK) |
| **Construction costs** | • Falling land, labour or material costs (US 1930s) | • Rising costs (Japan 1980s)<br>• Better-quality housing (France 1960s)<br>• Larger house size |
| **Mortgage availability** | • Higher deposit requirements (Netherlands 1980s)<br>• Credit tightening (Germany and Japan 1990s) | • Lower deposit requirements (Ireland and Spain 2000s)<br>• Credit loosening (US 2000s) |
| **Cost of financing** | • High real and nominal interest rates (UK 1989–92) | • Low real and nominal interest rates (UK 2011) |

fifty years' worth of data or in the five for which we can go back a century or more – we can see how wide a range of factors can drive what is happening to house prices. For most of us, though, our personal experience will cover only a handful of these factors.

**Table 9.2.** *Continued.*

| | Factors that tend to reduce house prices | Factors that tend to increase house prices |
|---|---|---|
| **Expectations** | • General belief that house prices will stay flat or fall (Germany) | • General belief that house prices will increase (UK) |
| **Taxation/ incentives** | • Higher property taxes (Germany) | • Lower property taxes (Spain 2000–2010)<br>• Tax benefits and subsidies for home ownership (Australia 2007) |
| **Alternative housing** | • Good availability of attractively priced, quality accommodation (Germany) | • Scarcity of rental property (Spain) |

The lesson from history is that we should be careful in making decisions based on such a limited pool of knowledge. By taking a tour of house prices through time and across countries, we have added to that pool. But there is one place left to visit. A place where house prices have risen as dramatically as they have in any other country: we will return to the UK.

# CHAPTER 10

## THE UK REVISITED

### MILLENNIUM REVIEW

IN DECEMBER 1999, TO MARK the turn of the millennium, *The Guardian* and the Nationwide Building Society conducted some research to see how house prices had moved over the last century.[1] They identified six houses that the forerunner of the Nationwide had helped finance the purchase of in 1900 and compared prices.

A terraced house in Dover had increased from £200 to £40,000: a yearly rise of 5.4%. A house in Hampshire jumped from £245 to £75,000, a yearly growth rate of 5.9%, while a property on a busy road in the Rhondda Valley in southwest Wales had risen by a more modest 4.9% each year, from £185 to £22,000. Three London terraced houses that had sold for between £237 and £300 in 1900 were valued at between £125,000 and £140,000 in 1999: an annual increase of 6.3%.*

Of course, these growth rates need to be adjusted for inflation, which averaged around 4% each year. For these houses the real increase over a century was around 1.5% each year, with the houses in London enjoying a stronger increase than the others. This in itself is intriguing because we know that the increase

---

*The price of an 'average' or 'standard' house in 1999 was around £75,000, so the houses in London were more expensive than average.

between 1952 and 2000 was above this at around 2.4%, which in turn suggests that the growth rate from 1900 to 1952 was nearer to 0.7%. Could it be that the longer history of UK real house prices is closer to the story we have seen elsewhere, rather than to the UK's recent increases of 2.4% per year since 1952 and more than 5% per year since 1995? But this analysis, based on a handful of properties, only whets our appetite for a closer look at historical house prices in the UK.

## LOOKING BACKWARDS

Now that we have had the opportunity to look at house prices in other countries over longer time frames, we can see how different our recent experience in the UK has been. But we still might be tempted to conclude that the UK is its own country with its own housing market. We are still unsure whether our grandparents and great-grandparents had a different perspective on house prices to the one we have today.

As we have seen, the longest active time series we have for the UK is the Nationwide House Price Index, which started in 1952. In this chapter, with a bit of detective work we will piece together data from several other sources to try to see further back in history.

## A HUNDRED-YEAR JIGSAW

It turns out that over the last hundred years a number of studies of house prices have been conducted: some cover only a few years, and some only one region; some are published, others are not; some are in old journals and books that have been largely forgotten, others are quite well known. But perhaps by putting all these pieces together we can build a history of house prices over the last century, as Robert Shiller has for the US and Nigel Stapledon has for Australia.

Our goal is to take an average house of today, taking the 2010 average from the Nationwide and Halifax house price indices, and then to estimate what a similar house would have cost at any point over the last 110 years. Where possible adjusted prices that take account of improvements in property characteristics will track this better. By using a number of indices and taking an average of them, we will also reduce any bias towards regions or house types.* And we can use newspaper articles and other commentary from the time to crosscheck the data.†

For the period from the end of the Second World War up to 2010 we can look to various government surveys, to the indices produced by the Halifax and the Nationwide, and to other published data. Transactions during the Second Word War were limited, but a number of lenders (the Cooperative Building Society, for example) recorded a valuation comparison for 1939 for properties on which they lent for transactions in 1946. This gives us the ability to extend our picture further back – to before the Second World War for the first time.

Before 1939 the data is more sparse. We can draw on the work of Professor Roy Wilkinson, of the University of Sheffield, who has reviewed the Registries of Deeds for a number of towns in Yorkshire in the 1970s and created an index of house prices adjusted so that they represented a 'constant' level of quality over the period.‡ In addition, Alan Holmans of the Cambridge Centre for Housing and Planning Research published a paper for the UK Treasury

---

*We have also seen that some series are adjusted for improvements in homes while others are just simple averages, so we need to either cross-check or adjust for these differences. Even those series that are adjusted (using the hedonic method, for example) may over time lose some comparability as some improvement such as running water or central heating become standard. For that reason, shorter time series that have less scope for a change in the mix of properties are more useful.

†See appendix B for more details on the sources and approach.

‡The registries for West, East and North Riding in Yorkshire were established in 1704, 1708 and 1736, respectively, but were all closed in the early 1970s. They contained a very large number of deeds relating to land and property, and a team of researchers looked at over 1.5 million deeds, extracting 50,000 valid data points.

looking at house prices in the 1930s. His data suggests that an average house sold for £590 in 1930 and for £600 in 1931. Prices then fell to a nominal low of £515 in 1934 before recovering to £545 by 1938. We can add these data points to the jigsaw too, along with an index of prices for new houses that was constructed by Dr Geoff Braae. In the early part of the twentieth century we can look to two studies of the ratio of house prices to rent levels: one from Alan Holmans and one from Professor Avner Offer of the University of Oxford. Other commentary and sources have been used to cross-check this data too: for example, information on the prices that local authorities were contracted to pay for a standard three-bedroom house from the mid 1920s until the Second World War.

One new series that has been created for this book comes from contemporary reviews of the property market published by *The Estates Gazette* and *The Economist*. These sources give a good sense of what contemporary commentators thought was happening to prices, with some reports mentioning particular price changes and others giving a qualitative view on house prices. Typically, these were compiled from a large number of estate agents writing annual reviews of business in their local area, and this also shows that beneath the averages each year there were both structural and regional changes occurring. Large estates were being broken up, and large houses were hard to sell. Smaller houses (or 'villas', as they are frequently called) were more saleable. Regionally, houses near growing industrial centres and those in or near London generally do better than houses in more remote areas, but in some years the fact that the London market was more dominated by investors made this market more sensitive to buyer sentiment and financial conditions.

## BRITAIN'S FIRST HUNDRED-YEAR HOUSE PRICE INDEX

When we knit together the various strands of data we can survey a tapestry telling us how the price of a 'standard' house has

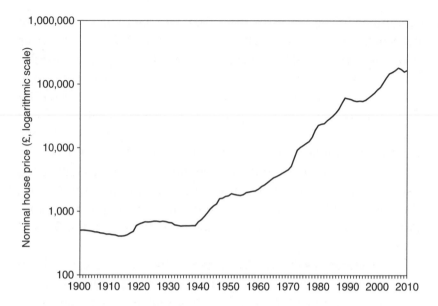

**Figure 10.1.** UK nominal house price index, 1900–2010.

changed over the last 110 years, and this is shown in figure 10.1. Our standard house cost around £460 in 1900 and then increased in value to £166,000 by 2010. That 360-fold increase over a century looks even more impressive than our recent boom, but we will of course need to adjust for inflation.\*

Adjusting these nominal prices for inflation converts the average nominal prices into the real prices shown in figure 10.2. In today's money, the price of our standard house was just below £40,000 in 1900 and £166,000 in 2010. This is a less dramatic, though still respectable, increase: a rise by a factor of more than four. The picture that emerges is quite different from the one that we have embedded in our beliefs – and it is a great deal closer to the one that we have seen elsewhere. Real house prices were at

---

\*Given the very large increase, the graph uses a logarithmic scale to make it possible to see the changes. The advantage of a logarithmic scale is that an increase of a certain percentage per year becomes a straight line.

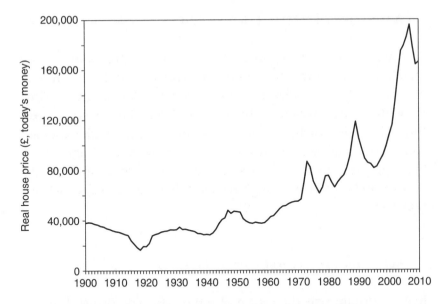

**Figure 10.2.** UK real house price index, 1900–2010.

about the same level in 1960 as they had been in 1900, two generations earlier. In the period before the current boom (1900–1995), real house prices rose at approximately 0.8% per year, whereas from 1995 to 2010 they grew at around 5% per year. It took over seventy years for house prices to double from their 1900 level, but that feat was matched in the nine years between 1998 and 2007.

It is worth remembering that we are trying to measure how the price of a standard, similarly specified house has changed over long periods. The average price of a house will have risen a good deal because the average house of 2010 is a great deal better than the average house of 1900. But we need to exclude this improving 'mix' effect to see the investment performance of an unchanged house so that we can compare it across time.

Now that we have constructed a broader real house price index for Britain we can look at the history of the UK in the same way that we were able to elsewhere, and we can try to understand why house prices were so flat for sixty years before rising slowly and then taking off in the last fifteen years.

## A HISTORY OF BRITISH HOUSE PRICES

A very large percentage, probably well over half, of today's commentary on housing talks about house prices, but this is a recent obsession. Many articles and books were written about housing throughout the last century, but until the 1960s there was precious little discussion of house prices. Before 1960 the major themes were slum clearance, improved sanitation, overcrowding, house-building programmes, the rise of building societies to facilitate house purchases by working people, and movements in construction costs.

### *Before the First World War (1900–1914)*

In 1900 Britain was the centre of the world. The British Empire covered a fifth of the world's landmass and was home to a quarter of the world's people. The population of Great Britain stood at thirty-seven million and there were around 8.5 million houses in England and Wales. In contrast to the imperial grandeur seen in many public buildings, such as the Royal Albert Hall or the National Gallery, some of these houses were very poor quality, and over the next few decades the programmes of slum clearance would be the subject of much debate and activity. Around 800,000 families had servants, many of whom lived in. The vast majority of people rented their homes, with only about 10% owning them.

Home ownership was also intricately linked to political power. Despite the Reform Acts of the nineteenth century, only around six million people, just over a quarter of those over twenty years old, were allowed to vote in Great Britain at the turn of the century, largely because they were male homeowners or long-standing tenants. Given all the rules, the actual number who could vote in practice was even lower than this. The First World War was to change this. After the devastation the idea that those who had fought and risked their lives for their country would be unable to vote appeared glaringly wrong. Starting with the Representation of the People Act of 1918, all adult males over the age of twenty-one were given the right to vote if they were resident householders and women over thirty who met some property qualification and were married to an eligible voter could also vote. The electorate in Britain tripled to over nineteen million. Now more homeowners were also voters and the fortunes of the housing market and the government were to be linked in a way that would change the shape of the housing market.

During the widespread celebrations at the turn of the century in 1900, many property owners would have also toasted the returns they had made in the strong property market that existed at the end of the nineteenth century. As the new century started, house prices maintained these new, higher levels for several years before starting to decline, at first gently and then more dramatically. Prices started to take a significant step down when Lloyd George proposed the People's Budget of 1909, which introduced a number of social measures that needed to be paid for by income and land taxes. With the richest 1% owning two-thirds of all property at that time, the members of the House of Lords would have been amongst the most affected by that tax burden.[2] They vetoed the budget, causing a constitutional crisis and leading to the removal of their veto rights in the Parliament Act of 1911, after which the Lords could only delay legislation.

With demographics changing as the possibility of living into retirement became much more likely, an old age pension was established for the first time, national insurance was introduced and the school-leaving age was raised to fourteen. Income tax was extended to around one million taxpayers, who were mostly the homeowners of the time.

Real house prices took another big step down in 1913 to a level about 20% below that of 1900, and at that time *The Economist* (17 January 1914) gently chided its readers when it remarked that

> owners who complain of depreciation are apt to contrast a price paid thirty years ago with what they can now obtain, without considering what they have derived from the property meantime, or allowing for wear and tear.

Meanwhile, social reformers were regularly pointing out the widespread poverty that existed and the very poor living conditions that many endured. These activists were joined by those who believed Britain needed a healthier, stronger population to maintain its empire.

Despite all this, the government played little role in the housing market before the First World War. When they turned their attention to it after the war, it would be to address the issue of housing people, not the issue of house prices, which would not feature on the government's radar until well after the Second World War.

### Homes Fit for Heroes (1914–20)

After the First World War the paths of government and housing were to become even more intertwined. The war had reinforced the belief that the population was badly served by its housing stock, with one poster at the time stating that 'you cannot expect to get an A1 population out of C3 homes'. At the same time greater political power was now in the hands of ordinary people, and that made housing an even greater priority for the government. The government had made a promise of 'homes fit for heroes' and now had to work out how to deliver that promise. The shortage of homes was to be a theme for most of the first half of the twentieth century and yet, as we will see, it did not cause substantial increases in house prices. Marion Bowley, a well-known housing professor, wrote

> For some years after the war of 1914–18 there were not nearly
> enough houses in Britain to go round. The rate of building was
> too low to keep up with the continued increase in the number
> of families.[3]

Following a buildup of public pressure, a Ministry of Health was established in 1919 and it quickly became responsible for improving housing. Back then, housing was seen primarily as an issue for people's health and wellbeing rather than being viewed in financial or economic terms. The state began building its own housing estates as well as subsidizing construction to the tune of around £260 per house built – around £8,000 in today's money. Between 1919 and 1922, when the scheme ended, over 200,000 houses had been built with these subsidies.[4]

House prices turned during the war, but it was not until 1919 that they saw any material increase. In that year *The Economist* noted that 'prices have gradually advanced during the year from 10% to 75% over pre-war values, [but] new building today is three times the cost of that prevailing in 1913'.[5]

By 1920, helped by postwar inflation, the price of a standard house had risen to around £625, but once we adjust for inflation prices had in fact nearly halved between the start of the century and 1920. This fall, despite the lack of house building during the war, can perhaps be put down to the grim fact that the war had ended with over 750,000 British deaths, with the influenza pandemic of 1918–20 causing further tragedy. Taxes had risen, hitting middle-class incomes, and investment resources needed to be channelled towards rebuilding the economy.

### Britain as a Building Site (1920–39)

In 1923, Neville Chamberlain (who had just become Minister of Health and would go on to be the Prime Minister) introduced a further subsidy for house building by offering £6 per year for twenty years, this time available for private companies. The first Labour government would extend this subsidy in 1924, under the 'Wheatley Housing Act', to £9 per year for forty years if the house was built for renting at controlled rents. This was partly to get more houses built but also partly to get more people into work by stimulating the building industry.

The 1920s were a difficult time for the economy, with unemployment rising in the early part of the decade and the rise of the union movement leading to disruption through strikes. This only got worse as Winston Churchill, then Chancellor of the Exchequer, tied Britain back into the gold standard at a rate that many felt was too high and would inevitably lead to deflation. Churchill's critics were right and the deflation that followed indirectly led to even higher levels of unemployment and, eventually, the Great Strike of 1926.

House prices followed these deflationary forces and fell in nominal terms through the interwar period from the nominal highs they had reached in the inflationary period of 1919–20. But, as we have seen with other countries during deflationary periods, real house prices actually rose back to their pre-First World War levels. It must be very hard for people to have interpreted these price movements at the time. Nominal prices had fallen from over £625 in 1920 to around £600 in 1933, but in real terms they had actually risen by 50%, and were back to their 1908 level. Even sophisticated investors would have found it hard to get excited about property as an investment.

The economic environment in Britain was already weak through the 1920s before the effects of the US Great Crash and the subsequent global recession made things worse. One of the benefits of the Great Depression, however, was that wages, and therefore the cost of building, fell, and because exports dried up many entrepreneurs started to look to house building as a profitable activity. This removed the need for the state to be the driving force in house building. Across England and Wales about 1.5 million houses were built in the 1920s, mostly with state assistance, whereas nearly three million houses were built in the 1930s, and most of these by the private sector.[6]

The 1930s also saw rapid growth in the building society movement, which financed around three-quarters of the new houses that were built. Mortgages started to take their current form – with terms extended from sixteen years to twenty-five years – and it became quite normal for middle-class families and even some skilled workers to be able to finance home purchases.

But this construction boom was not accompanied by increasing house prices. The price of a house in the late 1930s was around

£32,000 in today's money, which was about the same as it had been twenty-five years earlier. House prices had not crashed here (as they had in Paris, for example) and had therefore been a reasonable store of value, but anyone buying a house during this period in the hope of getting rich quickly would have been left frustrated.

Investors may have been disappointed, but the construction sector had played a major role in providing jobs, helping the country through the Great Depression. More than four million houses had been built, taking the housing stock from around seven million to eleven million.[7] The state, encouraged by the need to serve the broadening electorate, had effectively taken on the responsibility of improving housing. And improve it did. The historian Charles Mowat summarized an influential survey of the time as follows:

> In 1900, 26% lived in slum houses; in 1936, 11.7%. In 1900 only 12% had comfortable and sanitary houses, in 1936 at least 30%. By 1939 almost every house had its own water supply and its own water closet, and a third of them had baths.[8]

### The Second World War and the Return to Stability (1939–1950s)

House prices dipped at the beginning of the Second World War but started to rise again halfway through it. There was very little construction during the war, and during the blitz over a million houses were destroyed or damaged by bombs. Marion Bowley, who we met earlier, writing in 1944 noted: 'As everyone knows, the present war has led to a new shortage of houses. It is probably safe to say that the new houses needed ... by 1950 will be more than three quarters of a million, but less than one million.' It appears that the current belief that we have a shortage of houses appears to be nothing new, but in the past there was not the increase in real prices that we have seen in our lifetimes.

As the war ended housing was not prioritized as Aneurin Bevan, the postwar Minister of Health, focussed the attentions of his department on setting up the National Health Service. It was the Conservative party that pushed for more house building, with Winston Churchill, who was then leader of the opposition, proposing in 1950 that house building be prioritized ahead of the school-building programme: 'bedrooms before schoolrooms'. When Churchill was elected to serve a second term as Prime Minister, Harold Macmillan became Minister of Housing in the new government of 1951 and was given the task of building 300,000 houses per year – a challenge he soon met.[9]

Through the 1950s, 1960s and 1970s a great many houses were built, by all governments, both directly as state-owned housing and by the private sector. By the early 1950s nominal house prices approached the £2,000 level for the first time and prices were rising in real terms too. Having been broadly flat in real terms from 1900 until 1945, house prices were enjoying a postwar boom. They would fall back again in the early 1950s before starting the long, almost uninterrupted, climb to the present day.

### Onwards and Upwards (1950s to 1990s)

The picture from the 1950s is the one that we recognize from chapter 1, with slowly rising prices from the early 1950s until the mid 1990s.

There were three main cycles that occurred over this period. The first was the upswing in the early 1970s: this was a result of a boom in the financial sector that was eventually punctured by the OPEC oil price rises. These oil price rises triggered a banking crisis during which a number of banks failed, and as banks pulled back, and inflation soared, credit tightened. Real house prices swung up significantly and then dropped down just as swiftly. The fall in real prices resulted from nominal prices staying flat, with the very high level of inflation eating away at real prices.

There was a second, smaller cycle in the late 1970s, but again after an upswing house prices fell back as the economy deteriorated, with Britain eventually being reduced to asking for help from the International Monetary Fund. Once more, nominal prices were flat and inflation eroded real prices.

The third cycle saw real prices rise rapidly in the 1980s as financial deregulation saw a growth in lending and as interest rates fell. The Thatcher government believed strongly in encouraging home ownership and embarked on a programme of selling council houses to their tenants. The early 1990s again saw most of these gains lost as the economy faltered, interest rates rose and banks ran into trouble. Repossessions peaked at 75,000 in 1991, and by 1993 16% of mortgage holders (representing around 1.6 million households) were estimated to be in negative equity. Once more, while nominal prices did fall back the main cause of the fall in real prices came through higher inflation.


### Climbing to the Summit (1995 to the Present)

As we know, the period from 1995 to 2010 has seen an explosion in house price growth. Now that we can add the longer UK history to our analysis this increase looks even more remarkable.

It appears that several factors have combined to drive rapid house price growth since the mid 1990s, but with the benefit of a longer history we can see that not all of them are new. Demand for housing has grown as household numbers rise, as they have for most of the last century, while supply has been slow to respond, as has been the case at various points in the past. What sets this period apart is that investors/speculators have held a stronger belief that house prices would rise and they have therefore tried, desperately in some cases, to buy. Banks have facilitated this by relaxing deposit requirements and mortgage costs have been made more manageable by low interest rates and rising incomes. This system has become self-reinforcing as prices have soared.

The rise in mortgage debt over the early 2000s has been particularly striking. It took the mortgage market a hundred years to grow to the point where the sum total of outstanding mortgages was around half of total GDP, but in a few short years between

1999 and 2007 outstanding mortgage debt jumped to nearly 90% of GDP. There are three key factors in credit availability: the amount you can borrow relative to your income, the deposit you need to secure a mortgage and the interest rate you have to pay. The loan-to-income ratio jumped from around two times – a level it had been at through the 1970s and 1980s – to two-and-a-half times in the 1990s and three times by the early 2000s. With 10% deposits and 90% loans being the norm – not to mention the availability of the infamous mortgages that allowed loans of up to 125% of the value of a property – getting a mortgage was hardly difficult. There was even the emergence of a new sector of 'high-risk' mortgages to help deal with any difficulties.* Repayments fell too: in the late 1990s mortgage rates were around 8% but by the middle of 2003 it was possible to borrow 95% of the value of a house at a rate of below 4%, making it possible to fund much larger mortgages.

Where house prices go from here will depend on how these trends evolve.

## A NEW PERSPECTIVE

In chapter 1, we saw that real UK house prices had risen by 2.4% per year between 1952 and 2010 and by an even greater 5.2% between 1995 and 2010. With a perspective that now extends back over a hundred years, we know that real UK house prices rose by a much more modest 1.3% each year between 1900 and 2010 – and if we look only at 1900–95, this drops to 0.8%. This is much closer to the international comparisons that we saw in chapter 9, where across the five countries studied real house prices rose 1% each year between 1900 and 2010 and 0.5% for the 1900–95 period. Figure 10.3 shows the UK house price index against the average of the five countries since 1900. The effect of the small (0.3%) annual difference in house price growth compounds to a material

---

*High-risk mortgages have loan-to-value ratios of greater than 95%, terms of more than twenty-five years and/or income multiples above three. Of these, 45% were non-income-verified and 35% were interest only.[10]

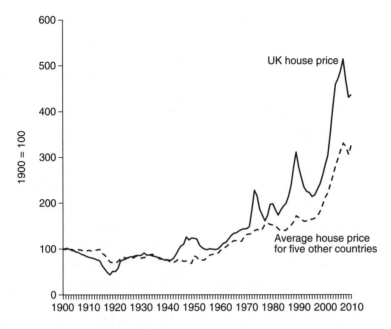

**Figure 10.3.** UK house prices since 1900 plotted against house prices for five other countries.

difference over a century, and most of the divergence appears to have occurred since the 1980s.

Our current 'standard' house has risen in today's money from just below £40,000 in 1900 to around £166,000 today. The cost of such a house would have been around £460 in the money of the time and you would have had to be quite well off to afford such a house. At the turn of the last century around 10% of the population were rich enough to pay the income tax rate of the day of 5% because they earned over £160 a year, and it would be this group that with a deposit of around £110 and a mortgage of £350 (2.2 times income) could have moved into our standard house.* Now, around half the population can afford such a house.

As we can see, the rise in house prices that we have experienced and our perceptions about how they change are at odds

---

*The 5% income tax rate was considered too high and was therefore reduced in 1907 to 3.75% on incomes below £2,000 (approximately £140,000 today)

with those that existed for most of the twentieth century. Our grandparents and great-grandparents would have had a very different view about how strongly you might rely on house prices increasing. We can see why house prices are barely mentioned in all the studies and articles about housing that came out prior to 1950s and 1960s. Indeed, when they were mentioned it was usually to point out that they were fickle and that houses were a risky investment.*

The story of much of the last century is not of huge price rises but rather of huge numbers of houses being built in Britain, with the number and quality of houses being transformed between 1900 and 2010. The story of our lifetimes, on the other hand, has introduced the idea of houses being a wealth-generating asset and the financial benefits of getting onto the housing ladder. With this longer perspective on the UK, though, our recent experience seems even more remarkable.

The next question is what this means for house prices in the future. We turn to this topic next.

---

*In his book written in 1965, *The Economics of Housing*, Lionel Needleman[11] wrote,

> There are considerable risks attached to investing in housing. The housing market is both unstable and unorganised. House prices can fluctuate violently and yet houses are much less negotiable than most forms of investment. It is particularly difficult to dispose of older houses, as building societies are often reluctant to give mortgages on older property. For the owner–occupier buying his house with a mortgage, a slump in house prices can result in the value of his house dropping below the unpaid balance of his debt. Apart from the chance of a general fall in house prices, there is always the risk that the particular house may fall in value. The architectural style may become less popular, or the whole district unfashionable.

And so he gloomily goes on for several pages. As he was writing, house prices were actually quite strong, but now that we can see the history that was his experience we can understand why his beliefs were very different from the ones we share today.

# CHAPTER 11

## WHERE NEXT FOR THE UK?

IMAGINE THAT YOU ARE SITTING in your garden in 2025 and your neighbour, or one of your children, asks you what you think about how house prices have moved recently. How might that conversation go? No doubt the UK will have changed dramatically in many ways: in terms of technology, in terms of our role in the world and the way we work. But there also seems little doubt that we will still be having the odd conversation about house prices.

We have seen in this book that trying to predict the state of the housing market in the future is nothing if not a fool's errand. That said, with the help of the industrious economists we have encountered, we have also seen how certain fundamental factors can drive what happens to house prices. So perhaps our route into thinking about that 2025 conversation is to outline three futures – three possible scenarios for what *could* happen to house prices over the coming years – and then to see which we believe is most likely. The one thing we can be certain about is that at least two of our scenarios will be wrong.

After trying to answer the question of *what* might happen to house prices over the medium term, the next question is, *when* might these things happen? Well, that seems too difficult. But there will no doubt be those who get the timing right, be it through luck or skill, and make a fortune.

## SCENARIO 1: BOOMING BRITAIN

Throughout this book, the search for insight into how house prices behave has led us to a wealth of historical records. Our investigations have shown us that house prices can move away from trend for very long periods, with a prime example being the boom in house prices over the last fifteen years in many of the world's advanced economies. One possibility is that house prices, having risen ahead of trend for the last fifteen years, simply continue to do so for another ten years, or even longer. There is no hard and fast rule on how long a boom can last, or how high prices can rise.

This presents us with a future scenario that we might call *Booming Britain*. House prices will continue to grow by 5% in real terms each year, meaning that house prices will be double their current level by 2025, surprising even the optimists. The dip that followed the financial crisis that started in 2007 will seem like a distant memory: a slight wobble on the graph of rising house prices.

How might this happen? As house prices continue to break records each year, nearly everyone will agree that the foundation of this booming market has been the unprecedented level of demand for housing that has existed since the mid 1990s.[1] In this future the UK economy will have emerged strongly from the financial crisis that started in 2007, and in particular will have outperformed its European neighbours. A significant number of workers from these countries will move to the UK in search of work, and with the weaker pound there will be many thriving companies in export-led industries that are ready to take on new staff. At the same time, the weaker pound will also lead to a drop in the number of people moving abroad as the dream of retiring to a sunny climate moves out of reach for all but the wealthy. With more people wanting to live in the UK, demand for houses will continue to rise.

Advances in medicine and economic progress will drive up longevity to new levels. Each year Buckingham Palace will mark a new record in the number of e-greets they send to those reaching their 100th birthdays. The new Dignity in Retirement Act of

2015 will allow the elderly to keep their homes even when they themselves have moved into care. This, combined with increased longevity, will mean that the demand for houses among this age group will reach new highs each year.

With strong economic growth, the banking sector will have recovered and been set free of the need for government support. Negative equity, bad debt provisions and repossessions will seem like relics of a forgotten crisis. Banks will have moved quickly from needing to strengthen their balance sheets to wanting to grow quickly, with bank bonuses and share prices dependent on doing so. There will be fewer mortgages as the number of transactions remains low, but each mortgage will be for ever higher amounts – and so each one will be worth fighting for. Interest rates will be kept low in order to boost exports and to keep the financing of government debt manageable, and, as happened in Japan, a 100% mortgage will easily be found at an interest rate of 2.5%.

With interest rates low, regular savings accounts will be an uninspiring place to keep any money, and with the spectacular returns that will have been made in property, many will choose to increase their investment in property. *Property Millionaire E-Zine* will have just written a feature article called *Palaces in the Stratosphere*, pointing out that the average house price stands at £520,000 (around £350,000 in 2010 money). With typical restraint, they implore their readers to 'board the housing rocket now for a journey to the stars'.

By 2025, anyone who has owned a house for a few years will have plenty to celebrate. The value of housing stock that had been worth around £4 trillion in 2010 will have risen to £8 trillion by 2025 – more if you include the effects of inflation. With prices doubling, anyone owning a house in 2010 will have made £165,000 in real terms over the fifteen years to 2025. That is over £10,000 in real terms, tax free, each year. As in previous booms, many people will choose to remortgage their houses in order to realize some of the gains in value, with the result that over 5% of all spending in the economy will come from that source.

Notwithstanding the favourable environment enjoyed by homeowners, there will, of course, be problems. Interest rates will be low, and as many homeowners also have significant savings there will be ongoing complaints that savers are subsidizing borrowers. And, of course, there will be the problem of whether their children, and the young more generally, will ever be able to afford homes of their own.

By 2025, despite the economy growing steadily and young people being able to find work, the rate of wage growth will have been far outpaced by the growth in house prices. Real wages may well have grown at the rate of the economy (around 2%) but with real house prices rising at 5% per year, the ratio of house prices to income will have increased from five times to nearly eight times. Average earnings will have tripled to over £75,000 (£50,000 in 2010 money), but with an average house now costing £520,000 (£350,000 in 2010 money), a £130,000 deposit will often be required. Some will look to support from their parents, but for most this increased deposit will often require saving for five or ten years longer than had been the case a generation before. Even then, the interest on a mortgage of £390,000 will need to be paid, and many a new homeowner will go to bed fearing that interest rates might rise: at 8%, interest payments would take all their after-tax income.

Unsurprisingly, the average age of first-time buyers will move higher. It was thirty-seven in 2010, but in this scenario it will reach fifty-two by 2025. A press release from the pressure group *Old and 'Omeless* will note that the extra fifteen years is mostly due to needing a higher deposit, partly because of higher interest payments, and partly because buying a house normally now comes after starting a family and paying off the costs of university loans.

This will create an unprecedented tension in British society between the young and the old, the haves and the have-nots. With half the electorate over sixty, it will be hard for politicians to work against the interests of the older (home-owning) generation. But many younger people will be angry that they have to pay high taxes, for care programmes and pensions that they themselves do not yet have, and higher housing costs. Many will consider emigrating and others will stay put and set up a new political party. After a number of wins in European and local elections, the Fair Deal on Homes Party will win its first parliamentary seat at a by-election in Cambridge, capturing most of the student vote.

Mainstream politicians will be divided over how to respond. Some will note that mortgage debt has doubled since 2010 and stands at two-and-a-half times the size of the economy. This group will worry about how this debt will be repaid. Low interest rates will make the debt manageable, but low rates will also be blamed for fuelling further house price increases. Others will claim that it is impossible to slow the process – arguing that the economy is like riding a bicycle and that any loss of momentum will lead it to fall over and collapse in a heap. Some will argue that the veto that local communities have been given on house building since the Local Democracy Act of 2016 needs to be lifted, but advocating such a measure, which would cool the housing market, will seem a sure way for a politician to lose their seat in parliament.

In among the social strife, many of those who had gained most from the rise in house prices will start to question their position. Their homes will be worth more than they had ever imagined, but it will require remortgaging or downsizing to release that wealth. Their own children will find it difficult to build lives for themselves in their own homes. At the same time, as they survey the economy they will see unprecedented levels of debt, and many sectors that will be dependent upon consumers continuing to remortgage to finance their spending, and this will make them worried about whether the strong economic performance will continue as they move into retirement.

This possible 2025 will present no easy solutions; indeed it will not be clear that there are any solutions that would not cause significant economic problems. The forthcoming 2025 election will, for the first time, see a major party campaign directly for younger voters – with pollsters predicting higher turnout levels among the young, compared with older voters, because of the frustration they feel. But the other parties will maintain their focus on the grey vote. When the results are counted we will see which course was the wisest.

## SCENARIO 2: BRITAIN'S GREAT PROPERTY CRASH

Looking back through history and across countries we can see that the past few decades have been extraordinary for house prices. Surely the rises cannot continue? Surely it is only a matter of time before house prices revert to trend – a process that some argue is already underway? In our second 2025 scenario Britain is recovering from the *Great Property Crash*.

House prices started to fall in 2007 and according to 2010 data they are 10% down in nominal terms and 20% down in real terms. For a while it will look as if house prices might stabilize at these slightly lower levels. But such hopes will be in vain. The huge debts that have accumulated in different parts of the world will start to create cracks in the global financial system. Many will have expected one or two peripheral eurozone countries to default, but the domino effects will be far worse than the central bankers had feared. The IMF will be forced to prioritize where to use its limited funds, and will have no choice but to focus on trying to stop the contagion – something that they will only just manage to do. Even in the stronger economies, such as France and Germany, almost all major banks will be forced to turn to their governments for support.

In the UK, several banks will be hit hard. With the sovereign debt crisis, and its associated write-offs, they will be required to raise further equity and they will be forced to pull back on their lending. Just when it looks as if the crisis can get no worse, the tighter lending environment will cause crashes in new areas. For example, in the huge commercial property market, owners of office, retail and industrial properties will be unable to roll over their commercial property loans. They will have no choice but to sell some properties to raise funds, and as distressed sellers and liquidators dump these properties onto the market, it will go into free fall.

The effect on the broader economy will be traumatic. With lending massively down, firms will struggle to finance their normal working capital needs. It will become increasingly difficult to pay wages and supplier bills – forcing many firms to pull back and focus their activities on whatever brings in cash the quickest. Economic growth will nosedive and a double-dip recession will ensue – and the second dip will be even more severe than the first.

Pushing the crisis to its nadir will be the subsequent collapse in house prices. Through the early 2010s, the banks will try hard to limit repossessions by switching troubled customers to interest-only mortgages and allowing interest-free periods. But many borrowers will soon be over twelve months in arrears, with very little prospect that they can ever catch up. Many homeowners will become trapped in houses that are worth a fraction of the mortgages secured against them. The ever-growing number of people in negative equity will find it impossible to move, even when work is available in another town.

House prices will have dropped month on month, but it will be the rise in interest rates will be the straw that breaks the camel's back. For several years in the 2010s not only will the government be pumping money into the weakest banks but the Bank of England will also keep interest rates very low – lower than they had been for centuries, and well below the rate of inflation.[2] This process that began in 2009 will continue to subsidize British banks as they borrow at low rates from savers and the Bank of England and lend out at much higher levels. But by 2014 the economy will have stalled, and the government will need to borrow money to cover its soaring deficit. When in October 2014 tax receipts fall 30% and social spending rises 10%, interest rates will be forced to spike up. Mortgages that had been affordable at 4% rates will suddenly become impossible to manage at the new 8% rate of interest.

The buy-to-let owners will break first. With personal bankruptcies reaching previously unseen levels the auction rooms will be crammed with receivers selling property. Buy-to-let magazines will soon be replaced on the shelves by new titles, with *Surviving Austerity* leading the pack. As mortgage interest payments are reset at the new interest rate level, over a million homeowners will stop being able to service their debts. In 2016 alone over £100 billion worth of mortgages will have to be written off by the banks. The spring of 2016 will be marked by street marches protesting at the dire state of the economy and in particular the high interest rates. With many unable to attend registering their protest via an e-petition, Downing Street's computers will crash.

But the sad reality will be that the banks will be unable to absorb this level of bad debt on top of the sovereign defaults and commercial property crash. By any normal measure the banks will be insolvent. As bankers and regulators testify before the House of Commons Banking Committee, it will emerge that none of their stress test models had considered a simultaneous collapse in the value of sovereign debt, commercial debt and house prices. Some outspoken CEOs will argue that even if they had modeled such a scenario, there was little that could have been done to contain it.

The government, with support from all political parties, will move swiftly to intervene, understanding that the toxic combination of a weak economy and individuals, banks and government all having unsustainable levels of debt will mean that falling house prices will pose a huge risk. Most of the second half of the 2010s will be consumed with trying to bring stability to the economy. This will start with the Emergency Financial System Act of 2015, which will nationalize the banks and introduce the Shared Ownership Scheme, with the government offering to become part owners of those homes where the owner simply cannot afford the mortgage interest. By 2016, there will be new controls on lending, new processes for repossessions and new initiatives to slow government spending. And it will work, with the economy returning to growth during the 2020–25 period.

But house prices will not fully recover. By 2025 real house prices will stand at half the level they had been in 2007. And yet not everyone will have lost out. After many years of rising, the average age of first-time buyers will fall back to thirty-three, and now with a steady job and a second income from a partner it will be possible for young people to buy a house if they choose. The idea that a house could provide a second income will seem like a distant dream – and a completely unrealistic one at that. Many will choose to rent rather than buy, feeling no pressure at all to get onto the property ladder – indeed the phrase 'property ladder' will seem very old fashioned.

It will be a hard couple of decades. The move from an economy based on property bubbles to a new economic model will require a major shift – analogous to the path that Japan will have followed some years earlier. There will be new opportunities as the recovery from the Great Property Crash gathers momentum, but of course that will be of little comfort to those who have spent many years unable to find work. After the big step down in economic output a key question will be how Britain can return to its historical growth path. The huge amount of debt that was still unpaid made it difficult to increase borrowing further. This will prevent the government from using deficits to stimulate the economy, and it will make businesses and individuals wary about increasing borrowing. While the recovery will show modest growth it will be insufficient to create a meaningful reduction in either unemployment or the levels of debt.

After significant cross-party cooperation during the darkest days of the crisis, politics will have returned to normal, with arguments as to who can manage different parts of the enlarged public sector more effectively. Alongside that issue, the campaign for the 2025 election will largely focus on housing and its role in the economy. One side will argue that the country needs consumers to spend more, which in turn will need people to feel wealthier, and they will point to the success of that approach in the late 1990s and early 2000s. They will propose policies that will lead to house price increases, the most striking of which will be their plans to demolish a quarter of a million empty flats. On the other side of the argument will be a group that will argue that inflating house prices is not a sustainable source of real wealth, and that the focus needs to be on investing in new industries. When the votes are counted we will see which course is preferred by the people.

## SCENARIO 3: LETTING THE AIR OUT GENTLY

Instead of house prices falling with a crash, they could do so gently and over a long period of time. As we have seen in this book, inflation can trick us by magnifying small real rises so they appear much bigger than they actually are. Maybe, then, inflation could trick us in the other direction and make a big drop in real house prices seem smaller than it is? If house prices were to remain flat – or even grow at, say, 1% in nominal terms – and inflation was, say, 4% per year, then after a decade real inflation-adjusted house prices would have fallen by about a third.

Our third 2025 scenario is of real house prices falling – not with the hard crash of the previous scenario, but rather as if inflation is the hot air that helps the balloon glide slowly towards its landing site. With inflation running at more than 3% in the UK, 2010 house prices are already 10% down from their peak in nominal terms and a more significant 20% down in real terms. Let us assume that nominal prices will spend a decade rising at 1% each year but, with inflation at an assumed 3%, they will in fact fall 2% each year in real terms. Then for the last five years up to 2025 they will grow at exactly the 3% rate of inflation – standing still in real terms but looking as if they are increasing in value. With the nominal price increases, houses will cost around 30% more in 2025 than they did in 2010 – or so it will seem. The real price, however, will have fallen back considerably, leaving real house prices in 2025 at about half their 2007 peak.

Current homeowners will lose a little bit of their real wealth each year. They will hardly notice this – with mortgage rates at 5% (2% above the rate of inflation), they will be able to manage the payments – but they will notice that house prices do not rise as rapidly as they had hoped. They cannot remortgage their houses to provide cash as their parents had perhaps done. Where their parents had looked to their houses to fund their retirements and care costs, that will now seem much harder to imagine. With a much more subdued housing market, it will be hard work for the average family to meet all their commitments and have enough left over to save for the future.

First-time buyers will become an increasingly large part of the market. By 2025 the average age of a first-time buyer will fall to thirty-one. Many younger people, however, will choose to rent rather than to buy. Many will prefer not to tie up all their savings in one investment in one city, when with cheap travel and an increasingly global workplace, the world will be their oyster. And they will of course listen politely as their parents talk about the 'good old days' when house prices could soar in value, but the conversation will move on swiftly.

Banks will spend much of the 2010s rebuilding their balance sheets, after the lending splurge of the previous decade. By 2017 all the banks will have paid back their government support. With low levels of repossessions and bad debt, banking bonuses will have been high for over a decade. There will be those who complain – particularly retired savers who will see their living standards fall as inflation and low interest rates for deposits erode their savings – but it will be as hard then as it is now to motivate people to go on a march to protest about these issues. Instead, their efforts will go towards being much more careful with their money. The huge popularity of the new book *Save a Million*, which will promise to help you save a million pounds over your lifetime, will show how keen many are to find a way to be both frugal and extravagant at the same time.

With inflation running at a fairly steady 3% the pound will take a bit of a battering. Foreign holidays will seem much more expensive than they had, and with petrol prices at an all time high, living standards will be squeezed. More generally, average living standards will have grown at their slowest rate for nearly a century. The level of individual debt as a proportion of income will have fallen by a fifth, but people will feel no better off. Government debt will also be stable, largely due to the fact that much of the outstanding government debt had been issued at rates of 3% or 4%, which with inflation running at similar levels meant that the government had very low real interest costs.

At the 2025 election, the main e-debate will become heated when the leader of the opposition uses the phrase 'Britain's lost decade' thirty-six times. It will be true that, relative to some countries, growth will have been slow, but the government will argue that Britain had fared well compared with the countries with equivalent mountains of debt, which had suffered real economic hardship. Some will argue that the costs of rebalancing the economy have fallen disproportionately on the country's savers, and in particular the retired; living standards will have stagnated for many years; and there will be the risk that inflation might soar. Unsurprisingly, others will claim that there was no real alternative: that the policies that had deflated the dangerous 2007 property bubble while maintaining employment and managing the large government deficits had been necessary. We will have to wait to see how the electorate judges these arguments.

### THE FUTURE STORY

So as you imagine sitting in your garden in 2025, you can test which of these scenarios seems most likely to you – and which seems most desirable. The future will almost certainly not conform exactly to any of our tidy scenarios, but the key questions will be partly answered by then. Will house prices have grown at well above inflation or not? Will there have been a sharp adjustment, a gradual one or no adjustment at all? Who will turn out to be a winner and who will end up losing out? How will we view our houses: purely as homes or more as investments? What is for certain is that whatever happens, there will be much to say about house prices.

# EPILOGUE

---

Over hundreds of years and in many countries round the world, fortunes have been made and lost in the property market. This is bound to be true in the future too for those who can time their purchases and sales well, and who take big enough bets. In a smaller way, those who have been fortunate to own homes over the last few decades have seen their houses increase in value.

Many have viewed this increase in wealth as coming for free. But, of course, there is always a cost. One part of the gain comes from increasing the amount of debt and risk that we as individuals have taken on. Another part of the gain comes from asking younger generations to pay more for the same house than today's homeowners had to, with some even being priced out of their chance to own their own home. The politics of allowing this transfer to happen have been attractive so far, as the winners have rewarded governments for their prosperity and as the losers have not held governments responsible for their need to reduce their living standards in order to buy a home. The ready availability of debt and low interest rates have helped to further disguise this transfer of wealth, as buyers effectively defer paying for these higher prices into the future.

The numbers involved are large. If real house prices in the UK had risen at 1% each year since 1995 instead of over 5%, the average house would be worth about half what it is actually currently worth. The average owner has received nearly £80,000 tax-free (but, of course, they need to sell to realize this, which is not so easy) and new buyers have had to find an extra four years' worth of post-tax earnings just to pay this capital sum.

As we stand at the latest peak in house prices, we should use this opportunity to reflect. What do we really want from our houses?

One of the features of the current housing market is that in most countries there is a significant policy effort to mitigate the impact of any fall. Governments that can keep their countries' interest rates low do so, and most use their influence over the banks to get them to introduce a variety of measures that support homeowners in financial difficulty.[3] Whether these policies will temper the size of the decline or whether they will simply prolong those declines, we will find out in due course. Many would argue that a long stasis in the housing market is unattractive because it means that the market does not reach its bottom for a very long time, thereby delaying the return of price growth and confidence. But maybe a few decades of gentle real decline is exactly what we need to make us reappraise our beliefs about houses as speculative investment opportunities.

While it is very hard, if not impossible, to predict short-term house prices, we have seen in this book that over the longer term prices can be swayed by the policy choices that our governments make: choices on mortgage standards and banking regulatory requirements, choices on levels of construction, choices on the tax treatment of property gains, and so on. It is our choice as to whether we use these levers proactively to influence house prices, but it is clearly disingenuous to suggest that we cannot have a big say in the future of house prices should we want to. Uncomfortable though it may be, it is time for us, and our governments, to decide what sort of housing market we want.

Most of us just want a comfortable and affordable home in which to live, and so we must hope that house prices will not keep moving out of reach for us and our children. But achieving the goal of affordable housing while at the same time avoiding the problems that a major crash might cause will require skill.

Perhaps even more difficult will be persuading the electorate that slower house price growth is in their long-term interests.


## PERSONAL THOUGHTS

Whenever I mention that I am writing a book on house prices, the first question has always been: where are prices heading? It is obviously a fair question, but it is a difficult one given how long house prices have stayed away from trend, in both directions, at various times. It reminds me of the famous warning from Keynes that the market can remain irrational for longer than most of us can remain solvent. Before I started researching this book, I shared many of the beliefs that I discuss in chapter 1, specifically about housing being a good investment, but I have come to realize how limited my experience has been.

If a friend asked me whether to buy property now, I would suggest that they look carefully at the long-term trends and, if they are buying in a country that is in the midst of a major boom, with prices well above trend, that they consider whether now is the right time. But houses are also homes, so they may end up buying even when they know prices may fall. If that were the case, I would suggest they are very careful about not taking on too much debt and I would suggest they make sure that they are buying for the long term.

If they are buying in a market that has fallen back, and is now near the long-term trend, then I would still suggest that they check that they are comfortable with the range of possible outcomes that are raised by this book. There is more margin of safety in buying at lower prices, but a low price does not mean it cannot become even lower, as we have seen. The risk involved in a long-term, conservatively financed house that you plan to live in, thereby avoiding rent, is quite different from that involved in a highly leveraged, short-term investment punt bought at the wrong time.

When I started looking at house prices, I worried that we were living through an unprecedented boom in many countries around the world, and all that I have learnt since then has confirmed that view. I suppose I thought it likely that the future path was for the growth rate to moderate. What has totally surprised me is the fact that real house prices in the US and in Amsterdam and in other countries have risen only very slightly ahead of inflation – not only over decades, but over centuries. This is simply not a paradigm that most of us even consider, let alone accept, and yet the message from the data is clear and consistent.

And whilst I can recall dips in house prices in the UK in the 1980s and 1990s, I had no expectation that house prices might be flat or decline for decades, as we have seen, for example, in Amsterdam. Again, this is a scenario we find hard to comprehend.

And, lastly, I did not expect that I would end up writing about the negative aspects of house price growth. I held the probably naive view that house price growth was 'a good thing', but as I have come to better understand the implications for those still to enter the housing market, I feel much less strongly that it is to our benefit as a society to have a set of policies that transfers so much wealth from the young to the old.

It may well be that the market will sort out a number of these broader issues in the years ahead, but I cannot help feeling that it will require some political courage to put the long-term benefit to society ahead of the short-term needs of getting elected.

Given the importance of our homes to how we live our lives, and the fact that they are by far our most important financial asset, there are four issues that particularly strike me from the analysis in this book.

First, we must navigate towards a more stable housing market, without having a damaging collapse in the market in the meantime. This is likely to require a continuation of the current relatively high rate of inflation, which will erode the real value of houses over time. In the UK, this process is underway, with real values down by twice as much as nominal values.

Second, governments need to decide if we would not be better served by a less volatile market, with less tendency to have booms and busts. It will require a coordinated policy encompassing the regulation of banks and of credit availability, management of interest rates and a more imaginative reform of planning that simultaneously enables greater house building whilst also protecting genuine community needs. These are all levers at the disposal of governments, but which will need to be actively managed for the long term.

The third issue is whether this longer history of house prices raises some uncomfortable questions about how much risk banks are taking in their huge mortgage portfolios. We now know that the risk taken on by banks is shared by all of us. Given that, it should be up to us to decide as a society, through our government, how much risk is acceptable – this can not be left to bankers alone. So we must hope that banking regulators' models are as rich as the range of experiences we have witnessed in our journey through house price history.

Lastly, we must decide how to balance the interests of housing the younger generation against the interests of existing homeowners. It is hard to see how this will not involve a significant growth in housing stock at prices that can sensibly be afforded by younger buyers.

My hope is that any reader who has made it to this point will have found the information about house prices that we have gleaned on our journey through different countries and ages to be useful. Perhaps it will also encourage some to ask our policymakers what their plan is. If it has achieved nothing else, writing this book will enable me to bore people at length at future dinner parties.

# APPENDIX A: LOGARITHMIC GRAPHS

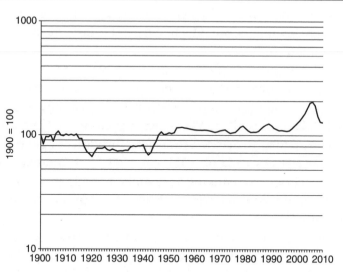

**Figure A.1.** US real house price index, 1900–2010 (log scale).
*Data sources*: Shiller; Measuring Worth.

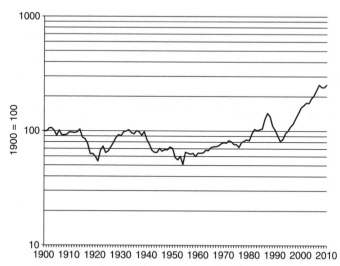

**Figure A.2.** Norwegian real house price index, 1900–2010 (log scale).
*Data sources*: Norges Bank; Statistics Norway.

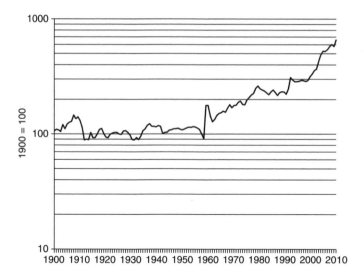

**Figure A.3.**  Australian real house price index, 1900–2010 (log scale).
*Data source*: Stapledon.

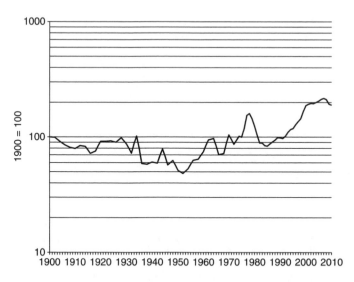

**Figure A.4.**  Amsterdam real house price index, 1900–2010 (log scale).
*Data sources*: Eichholtz; NMV; Central Bureau for Statistics.

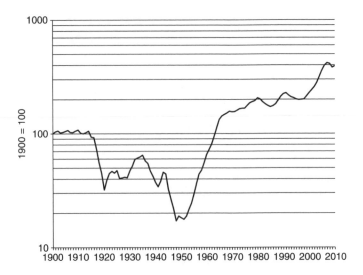

**Figure A.5.** Paris real house price index, 1900–2010 (log scale).
*Data source*: Friggit (CGEDD).

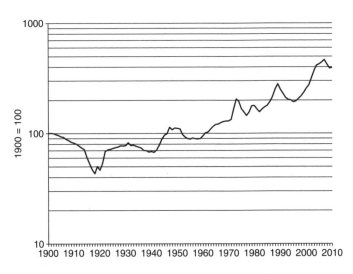

**Figure A.6.** UK real house price index, 1900–2010 (log scale).

# APPENDIX B: UK HOUSE PRICE INDEX METHODOLOGY

### OVERALL APPROACH

In order to create a house price index covering the period from 1900 to 2010 we need to rely on several data series, each with its own characteristics and each covering different time periods. This is similar in approach to the methodology used by Robert Shiller for the US and by Nigel Stapledon for Australia.

My approach has been to collect the data for the year-on-year percentage change for each index over a defined period. An average of these percentage changes has been taken for each year. This gives us an estimated percentage change in house prices starting with 1900–1901 and ending with 2009–10. Setting the 1900 price to equal 100, a nominal house price index for 1900–2010 can then be created. Adjusting for inflation gives the real house price index for the period.

### DATA SERIES USED BY TIME PERIOD

Working backwards from 2010 the following data series have been used to give year-on-year percentage changes in house prices. The years covered are shown in brackets after the name of the index.

#### *Department for Communities and Local Government Mix-Adjusted Index (1969–2010)*

The Department for Communities and Local Government has published a house price index adjusted for the changing mix in the types of houses sold since 1969. For 1969–92 it is based on the 5% Sample Survey of Building Society Mortgages. For 1993–2005 it uses another source called the Survey of Mortgage Lenders. And for 1995–2010 it uses yet another sequence known as the Regulated Mortgage Survey. I am grateful to the Statistical Office at the Department for Communities and Local Government for providing me with further data regarding this series.

### Halifax House Price Index (1983–2010)

The Halifax Index uses its own lending records. Their standardized index takes account of changes in the type, age, size and characteristics of properties to track the value of a standard house.

### Nationwide House Price Index (1952–2010)

The Nationwide Index goes back to 1952 and also uses its own lending records. The data since 1973 is weighted to take account of differences in regional prices, house sizes and types. Before 1973, only house size was taken into account.

### Department of the Environment BS4 Survey (1966–86)

The Department of the Environment 'BS4' Survey collected data from a panel of most building societies for a thirty-year period after 1956. It was developed with the Building Society Association, and a new approach covering most of the building societies' loans was introduced in 1974: this was called BS4. The Department of the Environment adjusted the figures back to 1966 to make them comparable with BS4.

### Department for Communities and Local Government (1946–69)

Before producing a mix-adjusted index from 1969, the Department for Communities and Local Government produced an index based on a number of sources. From 1946 to 1952 the series covers modern, existing dwellings with data coming from the Co-operative Building Society. For 1953–55 it is an average of two series of UK house prices. For 1956–65 it covers BS4 mortgage completions for new dwellings, and it is noted that new and existing dwelling prices moved in line with each other. After 1966 they move to the 5% Sample Survey of Building Society Mortgages.

### London and Cambridge Economic Service (1946–66)

*The Times* newspaper published an annual supplement for some years up until the 1970s with a data series based on average prices for a sample of houses sold with vacant possession.[1] The London and Cambridge Economic Service compiled the data.

### Nationwide (Spon's) (1946–52)

An index created by the Nationwide between 1946 and 1952 that was based on surveyors' estimates was published in *Spon's House Price Data Book*.[2] The index is split between modern and older houses.

### Spanning the Second World War (1939–46)

Measuring how house prices changed during the Second World War has a number of obvious problems.

Fortunately, we have six series where there is a 1946 valuation and also a reference to the 1939 valuation. This data includes an index compiled by the Department of the Environment Valuation Office, from the Co-operative Building Society Modern House Price Index, and from the Cooperative Building Society Older House Price Index. We also have a series from Alan Holmans of the Cambridge Centre for Housing and Planning Research with data for 1939 and 1946.[3] Professor Roy Wilkinson's series (see below) also covers this period, as does a series compiled by the economist Philip Redfern, whose data also takes us year by year through the war. Using these six series, we can calculate a ratio of the 1946 price relative to the 1939 price. Taking the average of the six data points tells us that prices increased by 119% between 1939 and 1946.

This 119% increase has been spread over the war years based on the shape of the Redfern year-by-year data set for 1939–46.[4]

### Braae Price Series (1923–38)

Dr Geoff Braae estimated construction costs for private homes and added in expected costs for land and builder's profit margins for the period 1920–38. We know that in the earlier years there was a divergence between building costs and house prices and for our index we therefore use 1923–38.

### Nevin/Holmans (1930–38)

Alan Holmans's authoritative compilation of housing statistics includes a set of hypothetical prices for 1930–38.[5] This takes the work of Nevin on loans made by the Halifax over this period, and the average loan-to-value ratio, and uses it to calculate the average hypothetical house price.[6]

### Wilkinson's Yorkshire Registries of Deeds Series (1900–1939)

In the 1970s Professor Roy Wilkinson of the University of Sheffield wanted to see how the housing market affected urban development, but he noted that it was very hard to get good data on house prices. He and his colleagues launched a very time-consuming effort to review the Registries of Deeds for a number of towns in Yorkshire.[7]

A team of researchers looked at over 1.5 million deeds and extracted 50,000 valid data points. Wilkinson then worked with this data to create an index of house prices adjusted so that they represented a 'constant' level of quality over the period 1900–1970.[8] This was important because, as one can imagine, there was a trend towards better housing during this period, and in particular a shift from back-to-back houses to detached or semidetached properties, with better bathroom provisions. Although the data is regional in that it is for twelve towns in Yorkshire – and we need to be careful about the extent to which regional prices diverge from national ones – its quality makes this very useful in providing a constant-quality index back to 1900. To reduce the effect of picking up a north–south mix effect, this data is used only up to 1939.

### Holmans's Years Purchase Study (1900–1913)

Data for house prices before the First World War is fairly sparse. One innovative approach has been Alan Holmans's creation of an index for 1895–1913 using a measure called 'years purchase'. This is the cost of a house divided by its rent, and it tells us how many years of gross rent would be needed before you paid for the house in question. Using years purchase data from A. K. Cairncross,[9] and rents derived from a book by B. R. Mitchell,[10] Holmans calculates a house capital value index.[11]

### Offer's Mean Years Purchase Data (1902–12)

Professor Avner Offer of the University of Oxford constructed an index from London auction prices that also used a years purchase methodology. His index is for 1892–1912 at five-year intervals. For our index, the sales weighted averages for leasehold properties for 1902, 1907 and 1912 have been calculated and smoothed over the intervening years.[12] This shows a much greater fall in prices in the run-up to 1912 than the Wilkinson or Holmans work. This may well be because the London market includes a greater proportion of investment properties – combining both series, therefore, covers a broader geographical mix.

## A New Series: The Market Commentary Series (1900–1925)

Most of the pre-Second World War data that exists relates to construction costs rather than house prices – the exceptions have been noted above. Whilst not a formal index, there was discussion in the press about the housing market during this period and I have constructed an index from this. To tie the commentary to some numerical data, these comments have been considered in the context of construction costs. These have come from Professor Karel Maywald, who published an important paper in the early 1950s looking at construction costs from 1900 up until 1938.[13]

*The Estates Gazette* and *The Economist* published reviews of the property market, and these accounts can give us a good sense of what contemporary commentators thought was happening to prices at certain times. These sources are especially helpful in the interwar period, where the construction-cost approach may not properly reflect house price changes. This is particularly true for 1918–22: during this period, construction costs tripled (before later falling back) but it appears that house prices only rose by around 75%.

We know that around 150,000 houses were being built per year at the turn of the century, but construction fell sharply from around 1904: to around a third of that level up to the First World War. From contemporary reports we can tell that house prices were running at levels below replacement costs, and they stayed at below cost levels until the 1920s. Construction rebounded in the late 1920s with government support. By analysing the commentary in these publications it is possible to construct an index that follows construction costs over the long term, but in a way that is supported by contemporary evidence.

Taken together, these various sources help us to map out the path taken by house prices in the UK over the last 110 years. If and when new historical information comes to light, particularly about the pre-1945 period, this will be incorporated and will be made available at www.safeashousesbook.com.

# ENDNOTES

For links to key sources as well as updates on the data when available, please visit www.safeashousesbook.com.

### Introduction

1. Partridge, E. (1972), *Dictionary of Historical Slang* (Penguin).

2. *The Mavens' Word of the Day*, Random House (www.randomhouse.com/wotd/index.pperl?date=20010611).

3. As noted on Michael Quinton's worldwidewords.org. See also Green, J. (2010), *Green's Dictionary of Slang* (Chambers).

### Chapter 1
### Are We As Safe As Houses?

1. There are a number of studies that show that homeowners plan to use equity in their homes to supplement their pension and pay for care in their older age (see, for example, National Housing and Planning Advice Unit (2009), Rapid evidence assessment of the economic and social consequences of worsening housing affordability, Report, Centre for Housing Policy, University of York).

2. According to Ratcliffe, A. (2010), Housing wealth or economic climate: why do house prices matter for well-being?, Report, Centre for Market and Public Organisation.

3. In England the median length of residence in one's current home is twelve years and the mean is sixteen years.

4. There are several possible ways to calculate average earnings. The Annual Survey of Hours and Earnings (ASHE) undertaken by the Office for National Statistics calculates that the mean gross annual earnings of everyone in employment in the year to April 2010 was £26,510. For full-time workers only, this figure rises to £32,178. But if you take the median (the earnings of someone exactly half way up the earning table), that salary is £21,221, or £25,879 taking only full-time employees into account. To be in the top 25% of earners requires an income of £32,665.

5. Just as the level of earnings is subject to some interpretation, so too is the price of an average house. This is discussed further later, where we will see that different bodies argue that in 2010 the average house cost anywhere between £162,000 and £231,000.

6. First-time buyers spend an average of 22.7% of their income on mortgage repayments, whereas for existing owner–occupiers the figure is 19.4%. (Source: *Social Trends: Survey of English Housing* (2010).)

7. European Mortgage Federation, Hypostat Report 2009 (published 2010).

8. In the UK, about 17.5 million homes are currently owner occupied, 3.8 million are privately rented and 4.5 million are rented from the social sector. (Source: Labour Force Survey, ONS, in *Social Trends: Survey of English Housing*. Data for the UK as of mid 2009.)

9. According to *Social Trends: Survey of English Housing* (2010), 13% of private renters in England expect to purchase a house within one year, 16% in one to two years, 32% in two to five years and 40% in five or more years.

10. According to a survey of young non-homeowners commissioned by Halifax, two-thirds of that group have no realistic prospect of owning their own home within five years. (National Centre for Social Research: *The Reality of Generation Rent*, May 2011.)

11. These are provided by Rightmove, going back to 2002, the Land Registry, going back to 1995, the Department for Communities and Local Government, going back fully to 1993, Halifax, going back to 1983, FT/Academetrics, going back to 1971, and Nationwide, going back to 1952. Each employs a somewhat different method in its calculations, and this leads to different outcomes. For example, Rightmove has a much higher average house price, and the Halifax Index shows a bigger fall since peak than the Nationwide Index does.

12. For a discussion of different approaches to constructing a house price index, see Wood, R. (2005), A comparison of UK residential house price indices, BIS Papers No. 21.

13. Halifax (2010), The UK housing market over the past 50 years, Report.

14. Adapted from data from the Office of National Statistics licensed under the Open Government License, version 1.0. (The same applies to the data used to create figure 1.4.)

15. The GDP data comes from the ONS YBHA data series.

16. This figure is based on the Barclays Equity Gilt Study (2011), which looks at investment returns since 1900.

17. Bogle, J. (2007), *The Little Book of Common Sense Investing: The Only Way to Guarantee Your Fair Share of Stock Market Returns* (Wiley).

18. Craig, D. (2011), *Pillaged! How They Are Looting £413 Million a Day from Your Savings and Pensions … And What to Do About It* (Gibson Square).

19. The graph is derived using data from *English Housing Survey: Headline Report (2009–10)*. Department for Communities and Local Government.

20. The Fathom/Zoopla Auction Price Index stood at 75.2 in February 2011, meaning that the average property at auction sold at a discount of 24.8% compared with the conventional market. This was not the case from 1998 to 2007

when auction prices were similar to, or in many months above, those in the conventional market.

21. Some believe that the rise in the number of two-income households has changed the picture, but in 2000/2001, 36% of owner–occupier households had two earners, compared with 36% in 1971, 1988 and 1991 and 37% in 1995. Conservative MP and government minister David Willets has pointed out that the proportion of first-time buyers that were single men in 2004 was similar to that in the early 1980s, while the proportion of single females had risen by 50%. The big fall was in couples: down from 315,000 in the early 1980s to 210,000 in 1995.

22. The Bank of England has tracked housing equity withdrawal since 1970. It started slowly, adding less than 1% to household incomes, but rose to around 4% through the 1980s and up until the 1990–91 recession, when it dropped back down below 1%. It then shot back up again to the 4–6% level between 2000 and 2008, before again collapsing after the credit crunch.

23. For a recent report, see Miles, D., Yang, J., and Marcheggiano, G. (2011), Optimal bank capital, Discussion Paper 31, Bank of England, External MPC Unit.

24. For 1977 and 2007, the figures come from GE Money Home Lending, while the National Housing Federation report tells us that the average age for first-time buyers without parental support is now thirty-seven.

25. Willets, D. (2010), *The Pinch: How the Baby Boomers Took Their Children's Future – And Why They Should Give It Back* (Atlantic Books).


## Chapter 2
## American Dreams and Nightmares

1. Tuman, D. (2011), White House real estate takes a hit – just like the rest of real estate, zillow.com, 6 January. See also, Tuman, D. (2009), What is the White House worth?, zillow.com, 8 January.

2. Lowenstein, R. (2006), Who needs the mortgage-interest deduction?, *The New York Times*, 5 March.

3. Shiller, R. J. (2005), *Irrational Exuberance*, 2nd edition (Princeton University Press).

4. This is similar in spirit to the later Case–Shiller index but is of lower quality as it is based on a survey of homeowners, rather than actual transactions data, and therefore depends on the accuracy of the owners' memories of original purchase prices and dates.

5. This data is taken from the prices advertised in newspapers, with an average taken across the five cities of Chicago, Los Angeles, New Orleans, New York and Washington, DC.

6. An excellent one-volume history is Hugh Brogan's *The Longman History of the United States of America* (1985).

7. The graphs in chapter 2 were created using house price data from Professor Robert Shiller and a consumer price index from Measuring Worth:

Shiller, R. J. (2011), Nominal house price index (available at www.econ.yale.edu/
-shiller/data.htm; breakdown: 1890–1933, Grebler; 1934–52, five-city median;
1953–74, PHCPI; 1975–86, FHFA; 1987–2010, S&P/Case–Shiller; the data for
1953–2010 was originally quarterly – an arithmetic average was taken to com-
pute the annual values); Officer, L. H. (2010), The annual consumer price
index for the United States, 1774–2010, Measuring Worth (available at www.
measuringworth.com/uscpi; based on BLS data from 1913 to 2010 and on other
sources for the period prior to 1913).

8. Bruner, R., and Carr, S. (2007), *The Panic of 1907* (Wiley).

9. Hyman, L. (2007), *Debtor Nation: The History of America in Red Ink* (Princeton University Press).

10. Black, W. K. (2005), *The Best Way to Rob a Bank Is to Own One: How
Corporate Executives and Politicians Looted the S&L Industry* (University of Texas
Press).

11. Lewis, M. (1989), *Liar's Poker* (W. W. Norton).

12. Immergluck, D. (2009), *Foreclosed: High-Risk Lending, Deregulation, and
the Undermining of America's Mortgage Market* (Cornell University Press).

13. Data from the United States Department of Agriculture shows that the
estimated real value of cropland per acre rose by 29% between 1997 and 2005,
but this does not explain why house prices rose more than 70% over the same
period.

14. Zuckerman, G. (2010), *The Greatest Trade Ever: How John Paulson Bet
Against the Markets and Made $20 billion* (Viking).

15. Rogoff, K., and Reinhart, C. (2008), *This Time It's Different: 800 Years of
Financial Folly* (Princeton University Press).

16. Ferguson, N. (2008), *The Ascent of Money*, chapter 5 (Allen Lane).

### Chapter 3
### Rough Seas in Norway

1. According to the CIA's *World Factbook*, Norway had a GDP per capita
based on purchasing power parity of $59,100 in 2010, making it the fifth richest
country in the world (after Qatar, Liechtenstein, Luxembourg and Bermuda).
The US is tenth, with $44,700 per person; the UK thirty-sixth, with $35,100 per
person. Back in 1819 incomes in Norway were at around one twenty-fifth of
today's levels.

2. The graphs in chapter 3 were created using data from papers by Eitrheim
and Erlandsen (nominal house price data for 1819–2003 is from Eitrheim, Ø.,
and Erlandsen, S. K. (2004), House price indices for Norway 1819–2003, Norges
Bank Occasional Paper 35, chapter 9) and by Grytten (inflation data for 1819–
2003 is from Grytten, O. (2004), A consumer price index for Norway 1516–2003,
Norges Bank Occasional Paper 35, chapter 3) and from information gathered by
Statistics Norway (house price data and CPI data for 2004–2010 is from Statistics
Norway (www.ssb.no)).

3. Gerdrup, K. (2004), Three booms and busts involving banking crises in
Norway since the 1890s, in *The Norwegian Banking Crisis*, edited by T. Moe,
J. Solheim and B. Vale (Norges Bank).

4. Øksendal, L. F. (2011), The margins for discretion: crisis management under a fixed exchange rate regime – the case of Norway under the gold standard, Paper presented at Past, Present and Policy: 4th International Conference (Geneva, February).

5. Based on an average of the first twenty years in the series (1819–39) to the last twenty (1990–2010).

6. This graph was prepared from data including some on real wages that comes from a paper by Eitrheim, Grytten and Klovland: real wage data for 1830–2003 comes from Eitrheim, Ø., Grytten, O., and Klovland, J. (2004), Historical monetary statistics for Norway – some cross-checks of the new data, Norges Bank Occasional Paper 38, chapter 7.

## Chapter 4
## Ups and Downs Down Under

1. These numbers are for the non-indigenous population that moved to Australia. In addition there were an estimated 350,000 indigenous people in Australia before this mass immigration.

2. Stapledon, N. D. (2010), A history of housing prices in Australia 1880–2010, The University of New South Wales Australian School of Business, School of Economics Discussion Paper 2010/18.

3. The graph in chapter 4 was created using data from a forthcoming paper by Nigel Stapledon: Stapledon, N. D. (2011), *Australian Economic History Review*, in press.

4. Wells, K. (2007), The Australian gold rush, Paper available on the Australian Government Culture Portal (www.australia.gov.au).

5. Simon, J. (2003), Three Australian asset-price bubbles, Reserve Bank of Australia.

6. Stapledon, N. D. (2009), Housing and the global financial crisis: US versus Australia, *Economic and Labour Relations Review*, 1 July.

7. Maslen, G. (2006), In the wake of the boom, *About the House*, September.

8. Stapledon (2009).

9. *The Economist* (2010), Floor to ceiling, 21 October.

10. Minack, G. (2008), Why I'm a housing bear, *Eureka Report*, 18 August (www.eurekareport.com.au).

11. See www.debtdeflation.com.

12. Stapledon (2009); Stapledon (2010).

## Chapter 5
## A Golden Age of House Prices

1. de Roo van Alderwerelt, D. M. O. (2008), Houses in Amsterdam: the van Alderwerelt family in Amsterdam during the 17th and 18th centuries, Paper on the family website at www.vanalderwerelt.name.

2. *Vier eeuwen Herengracht* (Stadsdrukkerif Amsterdam, 1974).

3. Eichholtz, P. (1996), A long run house price index: the Herengracht index, 1628–1973. (From 1973 the data is a broader index of house prices from NMV.)

4. van der Veen, A. M. (2009), The Dutch tulip mania: the social politics of a financial bubble, University of Georgia Working Paper.

5. Goldgar, A. (2007), *Tulipmania: Money, Honour and Knowledge in the Dutch Golden Age* (University of Chicago Press).

6. Chancellor, E. (1999), *Devil Take the Hindmost: A History of Financial Speculation* (Plume Books).

7. Shorto, R. (2006), This very, very old house, *New York Times Magazine*, 5 March.

8. For example, Marc Franke, Professor of Real Estate Valuation at the University of Amsterdam, has created an error-correction model to model house prices (see Franke, M. (2010), How bloated is the Dutch housing market?, *Real Estate Research Quarterly*, April 2010). His error-correction model has two equations: one that models long-term price levels based on factors such as incomes or interest rates, and a short-term model that looks at current prices versus predicted prices. His model suggests that house prices are a function of the costs of financing a mortgage, disposable household income and household financial wealth. Using these factors he models house prices since the 1970s, and argues that they are broadly at equilibrium today.

9. Xu-Doeve, W. (2010), The overvalued housing market in the Netherlands: a conspiracy of silence, IFC Conference Paper.

### Chapter 6
### Parisian House Prices: Eight-Hundred Years of Déjà Vu

1. d'Avenel, G. (1894), *Histoire économique de la propriété des salaires des denrées et de tous les prix en général depuis l'an 1200 jusqu'en l'an 1800* (Imprimerie Nationale et Ernest Leroux). Quoted in Friggit, J. (2008), Comparing four secular home price indices, CGEDD Working Paper, Version 9 (available at www.cgedd. developpement-durable.gouv.fr/rubrique.php3?id_rubrique=137, where you can also access Friggit's other papers).

2. Duon, G. (1943), Évolution de la valeur vénale des immeubles parisiens, *Journal de la Société de Statistique de Paris*. Quoted in Friggit (2008).

3. Ó Gráda, C., and Chevet, J.-M. (2002), Famine and market in Ancien Régime France, *The Journal of Economic History* **62**, 706–733.

4. Figures 6.3 and 6.4 are adapted from data from Jacques Friggit: Friggit, J. (2010), Le prix des logements sur le long terme ('Home prices in the long term'), Working Paper. Data available under heading 'Séries longues 1800–2010' from www.cgedd.developpement-durable.gouv.fr/home-prices-in-france-1200-2011-r137.html.

5. Friggit (2008).

6. Friggit (2008).

7. Friggit (2008).

8. Friggit, J. (2007), Long term (1800–2005) investment in gold, bonds, stocks and housing in France – with insights into the US and the UK: a few regularities, CGEDD, Version 4.0. Friggit uses a trend return for housing because the 1914–65 period is unrepresentative due to a combination of rent controls and high inflation.

## Chapter 7
## German House Prices: A Flat Story

1. Figures 7.1 and 7.2 were created using data from the OECD House Price Database (© OECD).

2. Germany has no single database for house prices. Instead it relies on a host of private companies, whose data is not readily available to the public and whose methods are not comparable and are of varying quality. The DEIX, for instance, is only a simple average of house prices, not taking into consideration the many differences between them. The OECD data that we use for the graph in this chapter comes from the Bundesbank. It does not use the 'repeat sales' method, instead relying on expert opinion to adjust for quality, etc. If houses have actually improved in quality, then the price trend may be even lower than indicated.

3. Burda, M. (2009), Half-empty or half-full? East Germany two decades later, VoxEU.org, 9 November.

4. Allianz Knowledge website: http://knowledge.allianz.com.

5. Michelsen, C., and Weiß, D. (2009), What happened to the East German housing market? A historical perspective on the role of public funding, Halle Institute for Economic Research (December).

6. Michelsen and Weiß (2009).

7. Michelsen and Weiß (2009).

8. Burda (2009).

9. Ball, M. (2011), *2011 European Housing Review*, Chapter 5: Germany (Royal Institute of Chartered Surveyors).


## Chapter 8
## Recent Collapses: Japan, Ireland and Spain

1. Hubbard, R. G. (2002), Impediments to growth in Japan, Keynote Address at *Fixing Japan's Economy*, 8 April.

2. Okina, K., Shirakawa, M., and Shiratsuka, S. (2001), The asset price bubble and monetary policy: Japan's experience in the late 1980s and the lessons, *Monetary and Economic Studies* **19**(S1), 395–450.

3. Figures 8.1–8.3 were created using data from the OECD House Price Database (© OECD).

4. Shiratsuka, S. (2003), Asset price bubble in Japan in the 1980s: lessons for financial and macroeconomic stability, IMES Discussion Paper Series, Bank of Japan.

5. Kanaya, A., and Woo, D. (2000), The Japanese banking crisis of the 1990s: sources and lessons, IMF Working Paper.

6. Okina, Shirakawa and Shiratsuka (2001).

7. Honohan, P. (2009), What went wrong in Ireland?, Paper prepared for the World Bank.

8. Kelly, M. (2010), Whatever happened to Ireland?, VoxEU.org, 17 May.

9. Kelly (2010).

10. Regling, K., and Watson, M. (2010), A preliminary report on the sources of Ireland's banking crisis, Central Bank of Ireland.

11. Keeley, B. (2010), The ghost of Ireland's property boom, *OECD Insights*, 30 July (http://oecdinsights.org).

12. Gonzalez, L., and Ortega, F. (2009), Immigration and housing booms: evidence from Spain, IZA Discussion Paper 4333.

13. Ayuso, J., Blanco, R., and Restoy, F. (2006), House prices and real interest rates in Spain, Documentos Ocassionales 0608, Banco de España.

14. *The Economist* (2008), Spain: after the fiesta, 6 November.

15. Cabrales, A., Dolado, J., and García-Montalvo, J. (2008), The Spanish trade-off: bricks vs. brains, VoxEU.org, 8 December.

16. McGovern, S. (2008), From boom town to ghost town, BBC News, 27 August.

17. Cabrales, Dolado and García-Montalvo (2008).

18. European Mortgage Federation, Hypostat Report 2009 (published 2010)

19. García-Montalvo, J. (2006), Deconstruyendo la burbuja inmobiliaria ('Deconstructing the housing bubble'), *Papeles de Economia Española* **109**, 44–75.

20. Kelly (2010).

21. Keeley (2010).

22. Kelly, M. (2007), On the likely extent of falls in Irish house prices, Working Paper 07/01, UCD Centre for Economic Research.

23. Latest prices can be found at www.permanenttsb.ie/aboutus/house priceindex/.

24. Ortega, E., Rubio, M., and Thomas, C. (2011), House purchase versus rental in Spain, Working Paper 1108, Banco de España. Sanguinetti, J. S. M. (2010), The effect of institutions on European housing markets: an economic analysis, Estudios Económicos 77, Banco de España.

25. Honohan, P. (2010), The Irish banking crisis regulatory and financial stability policy 2003–2008: a report to the Minister of Finance by the Governor of the Central Bank, Central Bank of Ireland.

26. Kelly (2010).

27. Blomström, M. (2002), What can Japan learn from the Swedish crisis in the 1990s?, in *Fixing Japan's Economy*, 8 April.

28. Blomström (2002).

29. BBC News (2009), Nikkei peak: 20-year anniversary, 29 December (accessed on news.bbc.co.uk).

## Chapter 9
### The Historical Picture

1. Figures 9.3–9.5 were created using data from the OECD House Price Database (© OECD).

2. Brinkley, M. (2011), *Housebuilder's Bible*, 9th edition (Ovolo).

3. Based on *The Barker Report*, which is discussed more later, with the average excluding highest and lowest country as potential outliers. Annual real increases in construction costs were noted as 2.8% for the Netherlands (1995–2002), 1% for the US, 0.9% for Denmark, 0.5% for the UK, 0.4% for France and −0.4%

for Germany (all 1991–2002). (See Barker, K. (2006), Barker Review of land use planning: final report, recommendations (HM Treasury; DCLG). Jacques Friggit notes that real construction costs in France rose by 0.6% annually between 1914 and 2010. For 1953–2010, where the data is most reliable, real construction costs rose by only 0.2% annually.)

4. Cahill, K. (2011), The great property swindle, *New Statesman*, 3 March.

5. Jacques Friggit notes that the Great Plague in Paris in the middle of the fourteenth century decreased the population by 30–50%. Between the second and third quarters of that century real house prices fell by 75%.

6. Duca, J., Muellbauer, J., and Murphy, A. (2010), Housing markets and the financial crisis of 2007–2009: lessons for the future, Spatial Economics Research Centre Discussion Paper 49.

### Chapter 10
### The UK Revisited

1. *The Guardian* (1999), Bricks are worth their weight in gold: a century of house prices, 18 December.

2. Lloyd, T. O. (1979), *Empire to Welfare State: English History 1906–1976* (Oxford University Press).

3. Bowley, M. (1944), Britain's housing shortage, Oxford Pamphlets on Home Affairs No. 9.

4. Bowley, M. (1945), *Housing and the State* (George Allen & Unwin).

5. *The Economist* (1919), Land and property in 1918, 11 January.

6. Becker, A. P. (1951), Housing in England and Wales during the Depression of the 1930s, *Economic History Review*.

7. Mitchell, B. R. (1971), *Abstract of British Historical Statistics* (Cambridge University Press).

8. Mowat, C. (1968), *Britain Between the Wars, 1918–1940* (Methuen & Co).

9. Clarke, P. (2004), *Hope and Glory: Britain 1900–2000* (Penguin).

10. Turner, A. (2009), The mortgage market: issues for debate, Presentation to the FSA Mortgage Conference, 12 May.

11. Needleman, L. (1965), *The Economics of Housing* (London Staples Press).

### Chapter 11
### Where Next for the UK?

1. Nickell, S. (2009), The British housing market: what has been happening?, *Oxonomics* (online journal).

2. Haldane, A. (2010), The $100 billion question, Presentation at the IRRNA Conference (Hong Kong).

3. Long, R., and Wilson, W. (2011), Mortgage arrears and repossessions, Report, House of Commons Library.

### Appendix B
### UK House Price Index Methodology

1. Alford, R. F. G. (1973), *The British Economy: Key Statistics 1900–1970* (London and Cambridge Economic Service/Times Newspapers).

2. Fleming, M., and Nellis, J. (1987), *Spon's House Price Data Book* (Spon Press).

3. Holmans, A. E. (1990), House prices: changes through time at national and sub-national level, Working Paper 110, Government Economic Service, HM Treasury.

4. Redfern, P. (1955), Net investment in fixed assets in the United Kingdom, 1938–53, *Journal of the Royal Statistical Society*.

5. Holmans, A. E. (2005), Historical statistics of housing in Britain, Cambridge Centre for Housing and Planning Research, University of Cambridge.

6. Nevin, E. T. (1955), *The Mechanism of Cheap Money* (University of Wales Press).

7. The registries for West, East and North Riding in Yorkshire were established in 1704, 1708 and 1736, respectively, but they were all closed in the early 1970s. They contained a very large number of deeds relating to land and property, and a small number of them contained information about prices paid.

8. Wilkinson, R. (1977), Trends in property values and transactions and housing finance in Yorkshire since 1900, Social Science Research Council Final Report.

9. Cairncross, A. K. (1953), *Home and Foreign Investment* (Cambridge University Press).

10. Mitchell, B. R. (1971), *British Historical Statistics* (Cambridge University Press).

11. Holmans (2005).

12. Offer, A. (1981), *Property and Politics 1870–1914* (Cambridge University Press).

13. Maywald, K. (1954), An index of building costs in the United Kingdom, 1845–1938, *The Economic History Review*.

# ACKNOWLEDGEMENTS

Creating a book from my original paper has been more involved than I ever expected, and one of the pleasant surprises has been the considerable help that I have received along the way.

I am first and foremost grateful to the researchers and economists who have worked on the complicated task of understanding the movement in house values over long historical periods. Bob Shiller's work in the US is the foundation for chapter 2, and his willingness to challenge conventional wisdom is inspiring. Piet Eichholtz has constructed one of the most fascinating historical series – that for Amsterdam – and it was this original work that challenged my preconceptions. I am grateful to Nigel Stapledon for his work in Australia and for generously allowing me to use his latest, soon to be published, data. Jacques Friggit kindly pointed me to the early French data, created the later French data, and has been extremely generous in sharing his knowledge and wisdom. Øyvind Eitrheim and Solveig Erlandsen's meticulous work in Norway has provided a rich story for their country. Without the work of these economists this book could never have been written, and I am grateful for their permission to use their research findings.

I would like to thank Karsten Gerdrup for his help on Norwegian financial history, Sebastian Seehusen, Christopher Rogerson and Cecilia Wiedeck for their assistance navigating the German housing market, Professor José Garcia-Montalvo for providing an illuminating insight into the Spanish economy, Patrice Ollivaud of the OECD for generously digging out older cross-country data, Jodie Grey of Barclays Capital for providing me with the Gilt Equity comparisons, Joe Cheung of the DCLG for helping refine some UK house price data for the house price index, Jeff Scott of Platypus PR for the photograph used for figure 5.4, and David Wood for his help in creating the website.

Each week I see additional information that I would ideally have liked to include in this book and my inclination is to procrastinate so I am grateful to some talented colleagues without whom the story would still be on scraps of paper and in odd computer files. I am indebted in particular to Bob Denham, who has been instrumental in researching, drafting and editing great chunks of the book. He combines an able economic mind with the ability to write in sentences. I have also been very fortunate to be guided by Romesh Vaitilingam of the CEPR, who has pointed me to relevant papers, works and experts as well as providing critique and direction in appropriate measures. Angus Foulis of the London School of Economics checked that I had used the right data in the right way and also made a number of valuable contributions to the story. I wish him luck in his PhD on US housing.

London Publishing Partnership has guided me through the publishing process, and I would like to thank Richard Baggaley for his flexibility and patience in dealing with a first-time author and Sam Clark for the care and effort that he has put into improving my original script, which I optimistically thought was closer to the finished article than turned out to be the case.

I have enjoyed the support of family and friends in writing this book and I would especially like to thank Victoria, Julie, Hugo and Laurence for putting up with me tapping away at the computer, and for volunteering to read proofs and even do some data entry. To pull together a story – with some analysis, some narrative and an overall message – is a skill I am continuously trying to hone. I have been fortunate to have had a number of gifted teachers over the years, including John Kendall-Carpenter, Walter Eltis, Norman Crowther-Hunt, Anthony Habgood, Barry Jones, Peter

Goldsbrough, Andre Perold, Chris Hogg, Kate Swann, Henry Elkington, Peter Williamson, John Donaldson, Stephen Bungay and many others who have helped me in different ways. I thank them all for making the time and the effort when they did not need to. Lastly, I particularly thank my parents for providing the supportive foundation from which I was encouraged to explore our intriguing world.

# INDEX

Page numbers in italic type refer to figures and tables.